Beautiful Boxes

DOUG STOWE

Beautiful Boxes

The Taunton Press

The Taunton Press
Inspiration for hands-on living®

The Taunton Press, Inc., 63 South Main Street, PO Box 5506, Newtown, CT 06470-5506

e-mail: tp@taunton.com

Editor: Christina Glennon

Copy editor: Marc Sichel

Jacket/Cover design: Rosalind Loeb Wanke

Interior design: Kimberly Adis

Layout: Susan Lampe-Wilson

Illustrator: Christopher Mills

Photographer: Doug Stowe, except for photos on pp. 165, 166 (top four), and 167 by Michael Pekovich, courtesy of
Fine Woodworking© The Taunton Press, Inc.

The following names/manufacturers appearing in *Beautiful Boxes* are trademarks: Ace® Hardware, Brusso®, Lee Valley®, Masonite®, Plexiglas®, Rockler®, Scotch-Brite™, Woodcraft®

Library of Congress Cataloging-in-Publication Data

Stowe, Doug.
  Beautiful boxes : design and techniques / author, Doug Stowe.
    pages cm
  ISBN 978-1-62113-955-3 (paperback)
1. Wooden boxes. 2. Woodwork. I. Title.
  TT197.5.B68S76 2014
  745.593--dc23
                          2014021693

Printed in the United States of America
10 9 8 7 6 5 4 3 2 1

About Your Safety: Working wood is inherently dangerous. Using hand or power tools improperly or ignoring safety practices can lead to permanent injury or even death. Don't try to perform operations you learn about here (or elsewhere) unless you're certain they are safe for you. If something about an operation doesn't feel right, don't do it. Look for another way. We want you to enjoy the craft, so please keep safety foremost in your mind whenever you're in the shop.

Dedicated to my sister Ann 1947–2013

ACKNOWLEDGMENTS

A GOOD BOOK IS ALWAYS A TEAM EFFORT, AND I AM
grateful for my team at the Taunton Press, including:

Peter Chapman for all his guidance from start to finish.

Editor Christina Glennon for keeping all my loose ends tied up into tight knots and bows.

Photo editor Erin Giunta for sharp eyes on everything visual.

Illustrator Christopher Mills.

And Art Director Rosalind Wanke for the beautiful cover.

In addition, but not least, I want to thank all my students from years of box-making classes, who listened carefully, challenged me to better explain myself, caused me to question how to best do what we must do, and asked me for my best efforts.

Contents

Create a toe turner

I TELL MY BOXMAKING STUDENTS THAT A good box can be a "toe turner." Artists tending their booths at craft shows have noted that they can pretty much mind their own business—reading, or quietly working on their craft, keeping an occasional eye on traffic passing by—until they see toes turning toward their work. This turning of toes is a clear signal, alerting the artist to look up from his or her work, make eye contact with a new admirer, and begin the process of making a sale.

We all want our boxes to be toe turners. We want them to attract interest from across the room and then sustain that interest as admirers draw close, as they visually examine remarkable quali-

ties and feel the fine textures we've worked hard to impart. Aside from the technical expertise we hope our boxes will convey, we hope that they will also convey a sense of good design and even of beauty.

There are two aspects to 3D design, and we must take both into account to create a beautiful box. There are aesthetic concerns such as how to make a box beautiful and interesting. Then there are practical or technical concerns such as how corners are to be joined, how various parts and components will work in relation to each other, and what tools and materials should be used. These concerns are not unrelated. The materials used can affect the lasting beauty of your box. The techniques used in making

a box, for joining corners and the like, will create a sense of rhythm, introduce contrast, or add texture to the box, with each increasing visual interest and proclaiming your craftsmanship.

One way to approach the aesthetic side of box-making is through the principles and elements of design, which have long been used by artists and illustrators to gain an objective view of their work and to improve its effectiveness. The *principles* of design are traditionally taught in art schools as unity, harmony, contrast, proportion, rhythm, balance, and visual illusion (effective surprise). These would be your design goals that apply to everything you choose to make. The *elements* of design, including line, shape, focal point, texture, color, and value, are *tools* that you can manipulate to make your work more interesting and more beautiful. And, just as these tools can be used by a painter or illustrator, they can help those who make boxes and furniture from wood. By studying the

application of these simple principles and elements of design, and by sharing these with my students, I've been able to improve as a creative boxmaker and have been able to help others to enjoy greater creativity in their work.

The principles and elements of design are easiest to understand when we see concrete examples of how they are used in making boxes. Each chapter of this book will address a principle or element of design and offer variations that will give you a better understanding of how your own exploration of design can benefit your work.

One thing you will notice is that there aren't enough chapters in this book to give each of these principles and elements of design a chapter or a box of its own. But the one thing about a well-designed box is that it will utilize all the tools available to the designer, though not to the same degree. For example, even though chapter 1 focuses on contrast, the box made in this chapter also utilizes line, rhythm, and other design principles and elements.

The boxes in this book represent my own continuing investigation of design, and I hope they serve you in the same way. Each chapter and each box shares some of my discoveries made in the pursuit of making beautiful boxes that I hope you will find most useful in designing boxes to suit your own creative pleasure.

Get making and have fun!

A Swivel-Lid Box

WITH THIS SWIVEL-lid box we'll explore the use of unity and contrast while designing a box. I used curved and angled lines in the lid to contrast with the straight, square lines used in the rest of the box. The pegs used on the flat planes of the lids and the different thicknesses of those lids also provide contrast. Unity is established by the common wood and the straight, lightly sanded edges used throughout. Variations at the close of the chapter explore more uses of contrast, utilizing the tool kit offered by the elements of design.

I teach woodworking to kids who are in first grade through twelfth grade at a small independent school, and wooden boxes are among their favorite projects, no matter their age. In my classes we use hand tools and nails because they bring woodworking safely into range for a less-experienced woodworker. Not all boxmakers start out with all the right tools or the working conditions to do more complex

work. Even if you have every tool in the book, you'll learn that working with hand tools offers special rewards. My kids learn, and so will you, that they don't need a fully stocked shop to make boxes, only a few simple tools. Pivot hinges, which we will use in this project, are a favorite at my school because we don't have to purchase or install complicated hardware, and the

result is a box that is both interesting and useful. This particular box can be made in a variety of sizes and proportions. Most importantly, its dimensions can be adjusted as it is made to compensate for errors in cutting parts to length or width. Through the use of the shooting board, cuts made off-square by inexperienced woodworkers can be fixed for precise work.

Swivel-lid box

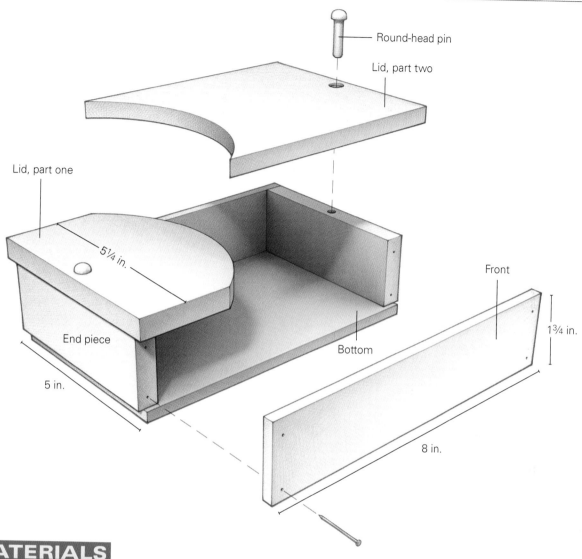

Round-head pin

Lid, part two

Lid, part one

5¼ in.

End piece

5 in.

Front

1¾ in.

Bottom

8 in.

MATERIALS

QUANTITY	PART	MATERIAL	SIZE AND NOTES
2	Front and back	Western cedar	¼ in. x 1¾ in. x 8 in.
2	End pieces	Western cedar	½ in. x 1¾ in. x 4½ in.
1	Bottom	Western cedar	¼ in. x 4¾ in. x 7½ in.
1	Lid, part one	Western cedar	½ in. x 5¼ in. x 4 in. Cut to 3½ in. radius, ⅜ in. from end.
1	Lid, part two	Western cedar	⅜ in. x 5¼ in. x 5½ in.
2	Round-head pins	Hardwood	7/32 in. x 1 1/16 in. Lee Valley® part number 41K01.02
12	Nails	Steel	1 in.

Unity and Contrast

UNITY AND CONTRAST SEEM TO BE OPPOSITES, yet both are simultaneous objectives of good design. How can this be? Contrast adds interest and excitement and leads the eye and hands to engage with a beautiful box. It can be achieved through the use of any of the design tools available to the boxmaker, including the use of contrasting colors, textures, shapes, and lines. Unity, on the other hand, is essential to good design because it makes the object seem purposeful and complete; it tells the viewer that there was careful thought behind its creation. Attention to unity expresses confidence, while a box that lacks unity makes the craftsman appear indecisive. The best boxes balance both contrast and unity to achieve something that is not only interesting but also feels well made with intent.

There are simple guidelines that I attempt to follow so that my use of unity and contrast each make a strong statement in the finished box. First, I make my use of contrast purposeful and informative. If there is a clear purpose for the use of contrast, it will not detract from the sense of unity in the box. On the main box in this chapter, the contrasting (curved or angled) shapes of the lids not only appear clever, but they also actually work well for opening the box and telling the user how to do so. The contrasting maple and walnut lids on the box offered at the close of this chapter also offer a guide for opening the box. A lid of contrasting shape and color as on the box in chapter 5 (see p. 74) hints at how the lid opens and where to put your fingers to open it. Miter keys of contrasting colors as demonstrated in boxes throughout this book highlight the craftsmanship invested in making a box. In other words, simply being different should not be the purpose of contrast. It is easy to get carried away into the realm of wishy-washy work by not paying attention to unity at the same time.

Unity is achieved through careful attention. For example, matching grain at the corners of a box builds a sense of unity, as does being consistent in the routing or sanding of edges. Unity is often the result of the consistent design decisions made by an individual craftsman. For instance, I've come to prefer a chamfered edge to the use of roundover bits when routing edges. Chamfered edges require more care in sanding than rounded edges, but I like the way chamfered edges look, despite the added care that they take. Being consistent in how you address the challenges in box design is a primary source of unity in the finished box. Find out what you like and what works well for you, and use those things to serve as the foundation for your exploration and use of both unity and contrast.

Some boxes are much easier to make with simple hand tools than others, and this box has evolved through years of teaching to give my students more immediate success. The ends of the box are thicker than the front or back. This provides more material in which to drive in nails without missing or splitting the stock. It also offers a place where the hole can be drilled to attach the swivel lid with adequate support. I made this box from widely available western cedar rather than hardwood, because softwoods work more easily and quickly with hand tools. Woods like white pine, spruce, redwood, and cedar are also much easier for kids to use and are more commonly available than many hard-to-find hardwoods. The 2-in.-thick western cedar I used for the main box in this chapter is available from my local lumberyard and may be found in yours, too.

In addition to this hand-tool version, I offer a machine-tooled hardwood version of this box as a design variation.

Prepare the stock

USE THE BANDSAW to rip the stock to preliminary size. This can be done with hand tools but requires greater effort and a secure vise to hold the stock.

1. Make your first cuts to prepare the 2-in.-thick stock using a bandsaw. Cut a 5½-in. wide piece to use for the lid and bottom with the remainder to be used to form the front, back, and ends. **(PHOTO A)**

2. Use the bandsaw to resaw the 5½-in.-wide piece into slices ⅝ in., ½ in., and ⅜ in. thick. The two thicker pieces will form the two parts of the lid and the thinnest one the bottom of the box after they've been planed with hand tools. **(PHOTO B)**

RIP A PIECE OF 2-IN.-THICK STOCK into thinner stock to make the lid and base.

THE PLEASURE OF USING HAND TOOLS

Many woodworkers with shops full of tools still enjoy using hand tools. Hand tools allow us to work quietly and to feel more physically engaged in the work. Using hand tools also provides a greater sensitivity to the quality of wood as the senses are better able to discern subtle things when the loud tools are turned off. The beginning woodworker can even get a better understanding of wood grain and its impact on the quality of work by using hand tools. For instance, a hand plane run against the grain makes for hard work, something that would be noticed by the woodworker. A power planer doesn't alert the craftsman to such things until later when the resulting poor quality of the planed surface is noticeable. Experience with the hand plane will teach you to take the time to observe the materials carefully and will help you to know what you're looking for to get the best results before your wood is fed into a noisy and powerful machine.

USE A PLANE to surface the stock smooth.

PLANE THE MATERIAL for the box sides smooth and square on all sides.

3. I chose to make the lid from two different thicknesses of stock, as the difference tends to hide any small discrepancies where they fit together and the two thicknesses are more interesting both to look at and to touch.

4. Mount the stock firmly to a workbench and use a plane to surface it, removing the bandsaw marks. Do this for each piece. **(PHOTO C)** While some of the box designs in this book require exact thicknessing of stock, this one, with its use of hand tools, is much less demanding of accuracy; and variations in stock thickness will not interfere with the success of the finished box. In fact, as I've learned working with my kids at school, minor variations from the original plan help to make each box unique.

5. After surfacing the lid stock, square the stock for the rest of the box using a hand plane. Make sure to remove the rough grain from the outside of the stock, and make it smooth on all sides. **(PHOTO D)**

6. After squaring the stock for the sides from the bandsaw, rip it into strips ⁵⁄₁₆ in. and ⁹⁄₁₆ in. thick. **(PHOTO E)** These will become the front, back, and ends of the box; and after finishing with a plane, the strips will be approximately ¼ in. and ½ in. thick.

PLANE THE MATERIAL for the front, back, and ends smooth, making each piece uniform in thickness. Minor variations in this box are OK.

Cut parts to length

A

SAW THE BOX SIDES to length; mark first with a square and cut with care.

1. Use a handsaw to cut the parts to length. Precise marking and cutting will make it easier to square the cut stock, so if you are a beginner, take your time and make a few practice cuts first. (**PHOTO A**) I use a Japanese-style dozuki saw for these cuts, but any saw with fine teeth could be used.

2. Use a shooting board (see the sidebar on p. 12) to square the front, back, and ends of your box. Hold the stock tightly to the cross-piece stop as you run the plane along the edge guide. After squaring both ends of the matching parts, check your work to see that both are the same length. If one is slightly longer than the other, take a few more shavings off it until the length of both parts is the same. (**PHOTO B**)

B

USE A SHOOTING BOARD to square the stock. Hold the wood tightly to the end stop as you move the plane along the guide strip.

A shooting board is a simple device used by woodworkers to square the ends of stock using a hand plane. It consists of a base that can be clamped to a workbench or held between bench dogs, a guide strip, and a stop secured at 90 degrees. To make one, I use a piece of ¾-in. plywood with a piece of thinner stock (either Masonite® or Baltic-birch plywood) glued on top. Square the stop using a carpenter square as shown.

To use the shooting board, simply hold the plane with its side flat on the base and with the cutting edge against the thinner plywood layer (see the bottom photo on p. 11). Hold the stock to be trimmed square and tightly to the stop. Move the plane back and forth, taking thin shavings until the edge has been squared.

Shooting board

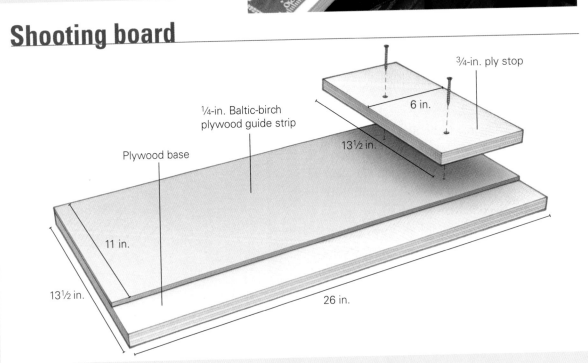

¾-in. ply stop

6 in.

¼-in. Baltic-birch plywood guide strip

13½ in.

Plywood base

11 in.

13½ in.

26 in.

Assemble the sides

A

GLUE THE STOCK INTO two "L" shapes as shown. Then when the glue has set, arrange and glue the parts to form the rectangular sides of the box.

B

AFTER THE GLUE HAS set, sand the surfaces smooth. Hold the piece with your hands low on the box to keep from tipping and misshaping the sides.

1. After the front, back, and thicker ends are cut into paired lengths, assemble them into "L" shapes, being careful to align the edges. For these, I chose to use gel-type super glue for a faster assembly time and so that the sides could be assembled without clamps. **(PHOTO** 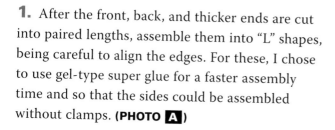**)**

2. After the glue has set (give it a few minutes), apply glue to the remaining ends and assemble the two parts into the rectangular shape of the box. Allow these parts to rest for 15 to 20 minutes for the glued joint to fully adhere.

3. I use a simple sanding board to quickly sand the edges smooth. **(PHOTO** **)** To create this sanding board, lay strips of adhesive-backed sandpaper edge-to-edge on a piece of flat particleboard to form a uniform sanding surface. Put 120-grit paper on one side and 180-grit on the other to make a two-sided flattening board.

WORK SMART

Adhesive-backed sandpaper on a flat surface works great to flatten the tops of boxes and to smooth edges without the use of power tools. You can stick the sandpaper temporarily to the top of the tablesaw or workbench or to a portable flat surface as was used here.

4. After the edges and the top and bottom of the assembled rectangle are sanded smooth, nail the parts together. One of the advantages of using softwoods like this western cedar is that it can take nails. **(PHOTO C)** Don't try this on hardwoods like oak, walnut, or maple without drilling pilot holes to allow the passage of the nails into the wood. You may use ⅛-in. dowels in place of nails, if you like, and either leave them raised as in the variation on p. 18 or sand them flush.

USE NAILS TO GIVE greater strength to the glued joint. As an alternative to nails, you can use dowels.

Attach the bottom

1. Cut the bottom stock to be smaller in each direction than the overall width and length of the box and glue it in place. For this box, I made the bottom ¼ in. smaller in each direction, providing a slight visual relief on each bottom edge. Again, I used gel-type super glue for fast adhesion. It has an additional advantage in this case in that when the glue dries, it will not be visible under an oil finish as would water-based glue.

2. Use spring clamps to hold the bottom in place as the glue dries. **(PHOTO A)**

GLUE AND CLAMP the bottom to the box sides.

3. When the glue has set, use nails to attach the bottom to the ends. You don't need nails on the edges where they are glued to the front and back of the box, because when edge grain is glued to edge grain using the same material, the glued joint itself is often stronger than the wood. **(PHOTO B)** If you want to add small feet to your box, use upholstery tacks.

USE NAILS TO PERMANENTLY attach the bottom. Upholstery tacks can be used to form small feet (as shown at right).

Put a lid on your box

Anyone who has worked with small metal hinges on boxes knows that there can be perils involved. Tiny brass screws are easy to misalign or can break. Working with kids, I needed a simple way to make lids that would open with ease but be hinged in a method that would be easier to install than tiny brass butt hinges. The swivel lid was the answer. But the swivel lid is not just a way to open a box; it is also a way to make the box more interesting in the first place.

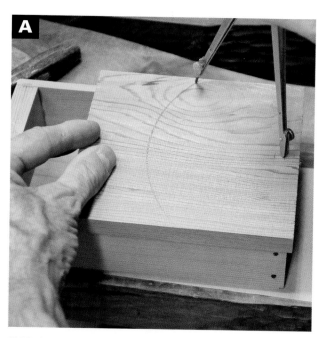

USE A COMPASS TO mark the shape of the swivel lid.

1. To install the lid, first decide upon the shape of one end. I show two examples (the second is outlined in "Make a Straight Cut Lid" on p. 18), and each is easily done. In the first example, the curved section of the lid locks the other section of the lid in place and must be turned open before the other end will begin to pivot.

2. Use a compass to mark a curved shape, with the point of the compass placed ⅜ in. from the end of the lid and at center. Scribe an arc. **(PHOTO A)**

This must be done before the hole is drilled for the round-head pivot pin to fit so that there will be material present for the end of the compass to fit into. The radius I used was 3½ in.

3. Use a coping saw or scrollsaw to make the cut. **(PHOTO B)** Clamp the wood firmly in a vise or to the top of the workbench and hold the saw so that the blade is 90 degrees to the surface of the stock.

4. Next, drill the holes for the pivot pins. If you have a drill press, you can accurately drill two step holes to partially conceal the pivot pins so that

they only appear as bumps on the top of the box. Set the depth to drill only ⅛ in. into the top of a lid part. Then use a 7/32-in. drill to finish the hole all the way through. **(PHOTO C)** Repeat the process with the other lid part. This same process can be done with a hand-held drill, but you have to take care that the drill is held vertical and not at a slight angle, which would make the lid pivot out of plane.

5. Drill the ends of the box for the pivot pins to fit. Make a mark at the center of the end piece. Set up the drill press so that the point of the drill is ¼ in. from the fence and it will drill into the center of the thickness of the piece. Drill to a sufficient depth for the full length of the pivot pin to go through the lid and full depth into the end piece. **(PHOTO D)**

USE A COPING SAW to make the curved cut.

DRILL THE HOLE in the lid for the pin to form the swivel hinge. The ⅜-in. drill fits the head of the pin; a 7/32-in. drill is required for the body of the pin.

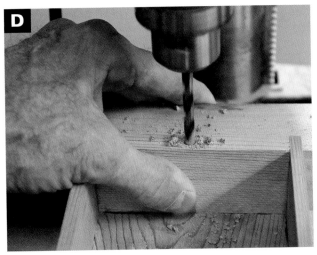

DRILL THE MATCHING HOLE in the box ends. Be sure to go deep enough for the length of the pin.

WITH BOTH LID PARTS in place and the shaped-and-sawn one overlapping the other, mark the line to be sawn on the uncut piece.

6. To mark the second part of the lid for cutting, attach it to the box and then overlap the curved sawn part next so that you can trace one onto the other. The pivot pins will hold each part in place. **(PHOTO E)**

7. After marking, use the coping saw or scrollsaw to cut the lid so that the two parts will nest together in the closed position. Check to see that they move smoothly in relation to each other and use a rasp or sandpaper to remove any obstructions to ease movement. You will note that I made the two parts of the lid out of different thicknesses of stock. This adds interest but also hides any minor imperfections in fit. **(PHOTO F)** Use a dab of glue in the pivot-pin holes and install the pins. Be careful not to use too much glue. It can seep out of the hole and glue the lids closed.

WITH BOTH PARTS SAWN, the lids will swivel open but only one at a time. Check to see that they operate smoothly in relation to each other. File, rasp, or sand if they don't.

Make a Straight-Cut Lid

AS A VARIATION ON THE CURVED-LID

DESIGN featured on the main box in this chapter, here's a lid-opening design that requires an angle cut. Make sure that the angle is steep enough to make the turn. If it is too close to square, the box will not open! A 15-degree to 20-degree angle seems to work well.

1. Cut one end, then, with both pieces in place, mark the other. (**PHOTO A**)

2. After cutting the pieces to length, sand the edges so that they are slightly rounded, except for where the thinner lid intersects the thicker lid. Only sand that edge lightly so that, when closed, less space between the parts is apparent.

3. When you have both pieces of the lid shaped and thoroughly sanded, use a dab of glue in the pivot pin holes and install the pins. (**PHOTO B**)

A SIMPLE VERSION of this box can be made with a straight cut. Simply lay one part over the other and mark the line.

APPLY GLUE in the hole to lock the pivot pin in place and secure the lid tight to the end of the box.

Build a Hardwood Variation

THIS SAME SWIVEL-LID BOX CAN BE made easily from hardwoods and in multiples if you use conventional power tools. Cut parts squarely and to accurate lengths using a sled on the tablesaw as demonstrated on p. 26.

If making this box with maple and walnut as shown, or with other hardwoods, much of the technique can be the same as with the swivel-lid box featured in this chapter.

1. Use two thicknesses of stock: thin for the front and back and thicker for the ends to accommodate dowels or nails for attachment and for the pivot pin to hold the lids in place.

2. Form "L" shapes with gel-type super glue, then assemble the Ls into rectangular forms. **(PHOTO A)**

3. Use the drill press to drill holes to uniform depths for the ⅛-in. dowels.

4. Round the ends of the dowels using sandpaper before they are hammered into place. **(PHOTO B)** If you choose to use nails rather than dowels and hardwoods rather than softwoods, drill pilot holes first or you'll end up with splits and bent nails.

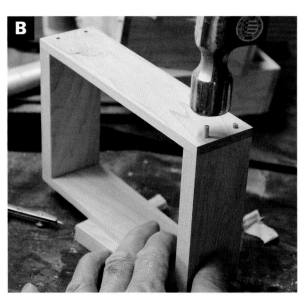

THIS BOX CAN ALSO be made quickly, easily, and in multiples, using common tablesaw techniques. Make a series of "L" components using glue to hold the parts in position.

5. I chose to make my hardwood boxes out of walnut and maple, using that strong contrast of colors to add interest to the finished box. Drill the pivot holes in two steps to partially embed the sides of the pivot pins. **(PHOTO C)**

AFTER THE GLUE DRIES and the surfaces are sanded smooth, drive dowels into drilled holes to lock the parts in place.

MAKE THE PARTS FOR the lid from contrasting hardwoods. I've used maple and walnut.

6. Instead of using nails to attach the bottom, first glue it in place with gel super glue and then drive ⅛-in. dowels into holes to attach it to the end boards. Glue alone will be sufficient attachment where the bottom meets the sides. **(PHOTO D)**

These boxes can be quickly made and display beautiful hardwoods, or they can be made with hand tools from softer stock. In either case, they should last for generations. **(PHOTO E)**

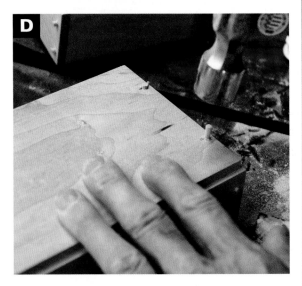

USE GLUE AND DOWELS to attach the hardwood bottom.

MAKE SEVERAL SWIVEL-TOP BOXES at once so you will always have a gift on hand.

A Lift-Lid Rectangular Box

IN MAKING THIS LIFT-LID box, we'll explore the use of line in box design. A box, just like any other work of art, is an arrangement of lines, planes, and focal points, and any small box can offer the boxmaker infinite options for playful development of new designs. Lines are used by artists to coax the viewer into engagement with the work. They also establish a sense of unity and direct the eye to important features. Good design keeps the viewer curiously engaged and wanting to touch.

While lines form the shape of the object, they are also visible in the structure of the wood. In this box, the sides are cut from a single piece of wood, with the lines of grain wrapping around each corner. Take the time to match the grain at the corners of a box, and you'll establish a greater sense of unity. You will also demonstrate that this is the work of a craftsman, and your careful attention will give your box greater value.

Making this box from white oak, I chose to use both straight and angled keys of contrasting black walnut to strengthen the corners and also to bring greater attention to the box's construction. More complex variations of this box offered at the end of the chapter illustrate alternate use of lines, planes, and focal point. The variations of this box hold a further surprise: a secret compartment within, concealed by a false bottom that can be detected only when the box is opened and its contents removed.

Lift-lid rectangular box

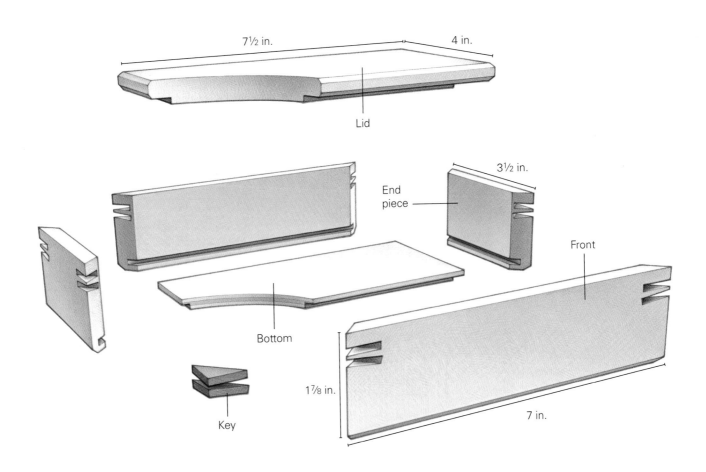

7½ in. 4 in.

Lid

3½ in.

End piece

Front

Bottom

1⅞ in.

7 in.

Key

MATERIALS

QUANTITY	PART	MATERIAL	SIZE	NOTES
2	Front and back	White oak	⅜ in. x 1⅞ in. x 7 in.	
2	End pieces	White oak	⅜ in. x 1⅞ in. x 3½ in.	
1	Bottom	Baltic-birch plywood	¼ in. x 3⅛ in. x 6⅝ in.	Includes ⅛-in. x ³⁄₁₆-in. tongue on each edge
1	Lid	Contrasting hardwood	½ in. x 4 in. x 7½ in.	
8	Keys	Walnut or contrasting hardwood	⅛ in. x ⅝ in. x 1¼ in.	Cut triangles from ⅛-in. x ⅝-in. stock

Line

LINE LEADS THE EYE IN THE DISCOVERY OF
form. Where lines intersect or run parallel to each
other or where they diverge, they give form to the
object. Sets of lines form shapes: For example,
three lines on the same plane can converge at
points to form a triangle. A chamfer is actually a pair
of parallel lines joined by the flat plane between.
Wood itself is a linear formation built line by line in
the form of annual rings. Some woods may have
indistinct grain, but in most cases the grain will be
worth noting. In those cases, the craftsman may
choose to match the lines of grain at the corners
of a box as a way of expressing care, inviting the
viewer to engage with the lines found in the wood.

Whether working in wood or on canvas, an artist uses line to direct the eye to a focal point or
points of interest in the work. In paintings, line can
give an impression of movement and relationship.
For instance, a line formed by a winding road can
lead the eye through a meadow, past a barn toward
the distant mountains. The same can be accomplished in a box through an arrangement of design
elements, leading the eye from one place on the
box to another. Lines formed at the intersections
between the various components of a box can also
provide information: For example, here is where
you lift the lid. An empty or negative space formed
by feet under a box might suggest: Here is where
you pick me up.

Some of the rules of line that I apply to my own
boxmaking are simple and are intended to create
a sense of unity and harmony in the box. I form
a routed line at the base to give the box a sense
of definition and weight. I try to be consistent in
the type of line I use. If using a roundover bit in
the router to shape edges, creating an indistinct
line, I use it throughout. If using a chamfer, I use
chamfers throughout, though all chamfers need

LINES OF GRAIN traveling around the corners of a
box tell the viewer that a craftsman's care was applied
in its making.

not form the same-size line. This creates a greater
sense of unity in the box and makes me seem
more confident and decisive. On the other hand,
I feel free to use curved lines to contrast straight
lines and to soften the feel of a box. I also pay
attention to line in my arrangement of pulls, lift
tabs, miter keys, and the like, as they will affect
the beauty of a box. For instance, a lift tab placed
in line with the miter keys at the corners of the lid
will look more intentional than one out of alignment
or off center. A craftsman's deliberate intention is
always noted, even if only subconsciously.

Prepare the stock for the sides

I PREFER TO RESAW MY BOX SIDES FROM thicker stock, using either the bandsaw or tablesaw, so that the thickness is in proportion to the size of the box. Resawing also makes thrifty use of stock. Of the two techniques, the bandsaw offers the safer option, but each will give similar results. After resawing, plane the side stock to a uniform thickness. When the stock is prepared to size (the sides of this box take a strip $3/8$ in. thick by $1\frac{7}{8}$ in. wide by 22 in. long), use chalk or pencil to mark the parts so that they can be kept in order for reassembly after they are cut. **(PHOTO A)**

NUMBER THE PARTS using chalk or pencil so they can be cut and still retain the lines of grain that travel around the corners.

Miter the corners

I USE A SLED AND STOP BLOCK ON THE tablesaw to cut the box parts to size and to miter the ends of each part to fit. But before you make your first cut on the sled, you will need to cut a piece of wood that can be used to vary the distance between the stop block and cut so that the long sides and shorter ends can be cut in sequence without changing the position of the stop block. To make this box, the spacer block must be cut $3\frac{1}{2}$ in. long, and use of it will alternate between cuts.

1. The first cut, with the inside face of the box down on the flat surface of the sled, is to form a miter at one end of the stock. Then the first part must be cut to exact length; this cut is made with the outside of the box face side up. A cut previ-

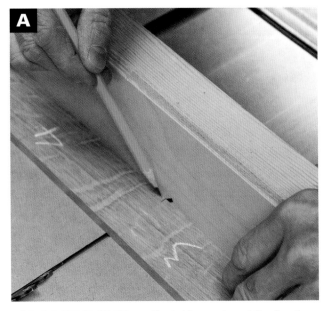

USE A MITER SLED on the tablesaw to cut the front, back, and ends to length. Align the measured mark on the work with the line of cut on the sled.

Sleds make boxmaking easy, safe, and accurate. Once you have set up a sled with a stop block to cut parts to a uniform length, you can make the same cut again and again all day long without any loss of accuracy. A sled also makes your boxmaking safer. It provides places to put your hands out of range of the cut, and, as you pull it back from a cut, offcuts are pulled back away from the blade so they can be removed without getting your hands close to the danger zone. I routinely use both miter and straight-cut sleds, and both are made in the same manner.

I prefer to use plywood as the base of my sleds; the proportions of the sled shown below will serve well in the making of sleds for any standard-size tablesaw and for making boxes of all sizes.

1. Plane material for the runners to a thickness that fits into the miter gauge slots on the surface of the tablesaw. A perfect fit with straight stock is desired, and it should slide easily in the slot, but with no motion side to side.

2. Rip that stock into two pieces equal in thickness to the depth of the miter gauge slots.

3. The secret I've learned to making sleds quickly and easily has to do with the order in which the runners are attached to the base and the direction the screws are driven into place. Attach the first runner on the underside of the base with a single screw, then use a carpenter's square to align the runner square to the edge of the plywood. Hold it tightly in position as you countersink and drive a second screw at the other end of the runner, securing it in place. I've found that two or three screws are usually sufficient for each runner.

4. With the first runner square to the base, attach the second runner from the top side while both runners are positioned in the guide slots. Apply paste wax to the runners for smooth operation.

5. After the runners are in place and the sled is sliding smoothly on the saw, add the front strip and hardwood fence using screws driven flush to the surface of the plywood from the underside.

6. When making the first saw cut into a new fence, carefully check the tablesaw to make sure that the blade is at the correct angle, 90 degrees for a common crosscut sled or 45 degrees for a miter sled.

While most tablesaws have blades that tilt to the left, sleds can also be made for saws whose blades tilt to the right. To make one for miter cuts on a right-tilt saw, position the longer part of the fence to the left rather than to the right and simply make your first cuts on the right side and keep the stop block on the left.

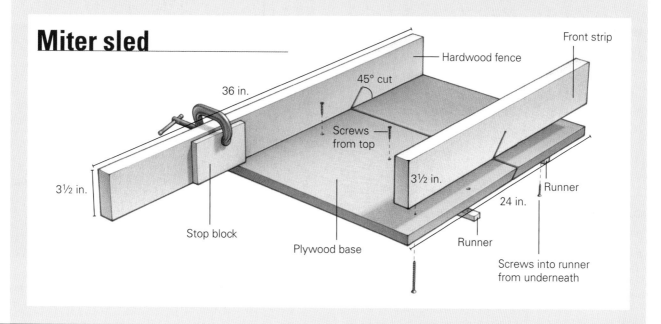

Miter sled

Front strip

Hardwood fence

45° cut

36 in.

Screws from top

3½ in.

3½ in.

Runner

24 in.

Stop block

Plywood base

Runner

Screws into runner from underneath

B

HOLD THE WORKPIECE firmly against the stop block to cut the first mitered part. Note the 3½-in.-long spacer block that will be used for the alternating cuts.

ously made on the sled shows exactly where the blade will cut the wood. (**PHOTO A on p. 24**) I use a tape measure and pencil to mark the length of the first long part, align that mark with the cut in the sled, and clamp a stop block in place.

2. Make the first cut with the box front or back held tightly against the stop block. (**PHOTO B**) Then, to cut the next matching part, flip the stock upside down and make a fresh mitered cut with the outside face of the box down. You could avoid this cut if you were not concerned with matching grain on the outside of the box; but if you want to align grain at the corners it is necessary to have a fresh miter at each end, cut in the proper sequence.

3. Put the 3½-in.-long spacer block in place to reduce the distance between the stop block and the line of cut. Slide the second piece in place against the spacer block and cut with the second piece held on the sled with the outside face up.

C

USE THE SPACER BLOCK to shorten the distance between the stop block and blade as you cut the ends.

D

TAPE THE FRONT, back, and ends with masking tape, aligning the grain as it was in the original wood.

4. To cut the remaining two pieces, follow the same sequence of cuts. The next cut will be made first, outside face down to miter the end, then, outside face up with the spacer block removed and the end held tightly against the stop block.

5. To make the final box end, make a trimming cut first with the stock outside face down. Then

with the spacer block in place and the outside face up, make the last cut. **(PHOTO C)**

6. Use tape at the corners for a trial assembly of your box to see that the miters are a perfect fit. **(PHOTO D)**

Fit the bottom

BECAUSE OF POSSIBLE VARIATIONS in measurements and the final planed thickness of the box sides, it is best to determine the actual size of the bottom of your box by measuring.

1. With the box sides taped together, measure the inside distances from one end to the other and from the front to back of the trial-assembled box. **(PHOTO A)** To determine the size of the bottom, add ⅜ in. to each dimension to allow for a ³⁄₁₆-in. tongue on each edge.

2. Cut Baltic-birch plywood to size for the bottom. Use the ripping fence on the tablesaw to cut it to precise width and then the crosscut sled on the tablesaw to cut it to precise length. **(PHOTO B)** You can make the bottom from either ⅛-in. or ¼-in. stock; the ¼-in. material requires a couple of more steps but makes a box that is flush on the bottom.

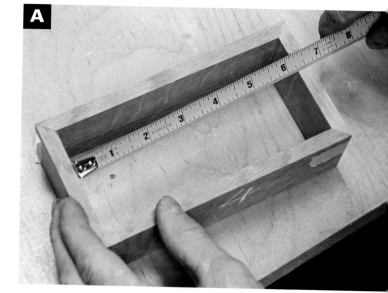

MEASURE THE INSIDE of the box to determine the size of the box bottom; add ⅜ in. to each dimension for the tongues that will fit into the box sides.

USE A CROSSCUT SLED on the tablesaw to cut the Baltic-birch plywood bottom to length.

3. The next step is the same for either the ⅛-in. or ¼-in. stock. Set the height of the tablesaw blade at ³⁄₁₆ in. **(PHOTO C)**

4. Set the fence ⅛ in. away from the blade and pass each box side through the cut, using a push stick to hold it firmly down on the tablesaw. Make certain that the bottom edge of each piece is against the fence for this operation. **(PHOTO D)**

5. If using ¼-in. ply, trim around the edges of the bottom material to make the edges thin enough to fit the grooves cut in each side. (This step is

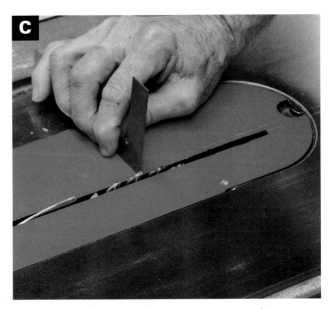

CAREFULLY SET THE BLADE HEIGHT at ³⁄₁₆ in., half the thickness of the box sides.

not necessary if using ⅛-in. ply for the bottom of your box.) Again, a blade with a square-top cut will work best. Use a push stick flat on the table-saw to guide the stock safely through the cut while keeping your hands a safe distance from the blade. **(PHOTO E)**

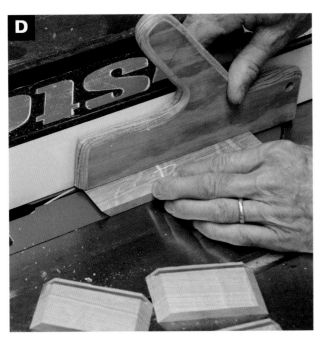

SET THE FENCE so that the space between it and the blade is ⅛ in. Then use a notched push stick to guide the box sides through the cut.

For cutting grooves and forming panels, I use a blade that has a square-top cut, which makes the measuring and fit easy. If you use a blade with a crowned cut, you will need to measure the height of the blade above the saw from the low point rather than the high point of the cut.

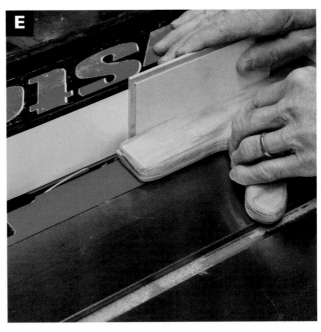

FORM THE TONGUES on the Baltic-birch plywood with the same setup used for cutting the grooves in the sides. Use the same push stick to hold the stock tightly to the fence while keeping your hands at a safe distance from the blade.

Assemble the box

A

USE A SQUEEZE BOTTLE to apply glue to the mitered surfaces and just a bit of glue at the ends of the grooves to lock the bottom panel in place. The corners are held together at this point with masking tape.

1. Begin by taping the ends of the box parts together, being careful to reassemble them in the order they were first cut.

2. Apply glue to each mitered surface. I use a small accordion squeeze bottle to apply just the right amount of glue. Because the plywood bot-

B

ROLL THE BOX SIDES around the bottom as you assemble it.

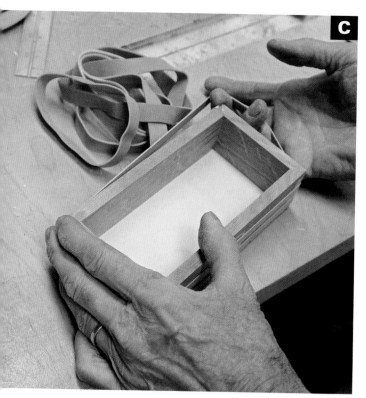

C

tom of this box will not expand and contract, a bit of glue placed in the grooves in the sides gives strength to the finished box. **(PHOTO A)**

3. Simply "roll" the box sides around the bottom panel to assemble the box. **(PHOTO B)**

4. If the joints are well cut, rubber bands will apply enough pressure to hold the corners in alignment as the glue sets. **(PHOTO C)**

LARGE RUBBER BANDS make great clamps for small boxes. Apply several to build up clamping pressure.

Cutting thin slots at the corners of small boxes to fit keys of contrasting wood to strengthen mitered joints and add visual interest is easy with this jig. The body of the jig slides along the fence and the supports hold the box at a 45-degree angle as it crosses the blade. I made this one with a small lip on the back that hangs over the edge of the tablesaw fence to keep it tight to the fence as it slides back and forth through the cut.

Cut your stock for the body of the jig from scrap plywood or MDF. Use ¾-in. stock to form the two parts of the cradle. Use screws to attach the parts so the jig can be taken apart and modified later and so that the parts can be replaced without wasting the body of the jig. Be certain, however, that the screws are positioned at a height where they will not contact the blade.

This keyed miter guide can be used for any box that is small and easy to handle and that has its miter keys located fairly close to the top or bottom edge. Another sled with the same purpose is shown on p. 49. I use a jig made in exactly the same way to cut deeper grooves when making a lid for a box (see the steps on p. 104 in "A Finger-Jointed Chest").

Keyed miter guide

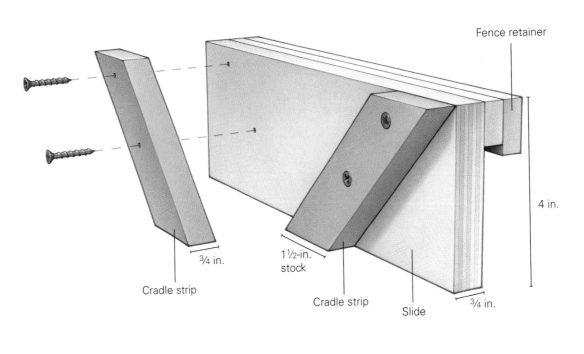

Fence retainer

¾ in.

Cradle strip

1½-in. stock

Cradle strip

Slide

¾ in.

4 in.

Install the miter keys

A SIMPLE JIG made to slide along the tablesaw fence holds the box in position as the miter-key slots are cut. I make two cuts in each corner; the first straight and the second farther from the top edge and angled at 8 degrees to add interest. (While this jig is slightly different from the one on the facing page, it operates in the same way.)

I USE KEYS IN A WOOD OF A CONTRASTING COLOR to strengthen the corners of this box. The simple jig shown on the facing page follows along the tablesaw fence and holds the box at just the right angle to make this cut.

1. Make the first cuts with the tablesaw blade raised to a height of about ⅝ in. **(PHOTO A)** Cut each of the four corners the same way.

2. To make the second angled cuts, move the fence over about ¼ in. and tilt the blade at an 8-degree angle. Putting these two keys at different angles is visually interesting and also adds greater strength to the joint.

3. To make the miter keys in sufficient quantities for several boxes, I rip walnut into thin strips sized to fit the keys exactly. Apply masking tape to make a tight bundle of strips. Then use the tablesaw and a 45-degree angle sled to cut packets of triangle-shaped keys. **(PHOTO B)** With the strips on edge, make one cut and then the next, flipping

MAKE THE KEYS from ⅛-in.-thick contrasting hardwood, bundled with tape so that several can be safely cut at the same time on the miter sled. Flip the bundle one way and then the other to form triangular keys.

the bundle over between cuts. Not all of these keys will offer a perfect fit. Sand down or throw away those that are too thick, and throw out those that are too thin.

4. Use a squeeze bottle to apply just a bit of glue in the miter key slots and on each key before it is pushed into place. A perfect fit is one that can be pushed into place without needing to be struck with a hammer or mallet. **(PHOTO C)**

5. After the keys have been glued in place, sand them flush with the box sides. I frequently do this with a 6-in. by 48-in. stationary belt sander, but it can also be done with self-adhesive sandpaper glued to a flat surface as shown on p. 13.

6. The next step is important to create a sense of unity in the finished box. A small routed chamfer along the bottom edge gives a point of separation between the box and the table, shelf, or desk upon which it may rest. To cut the chamfer, use a 45-degree chamfering router bit with the cutting edge raised about ⅛ in. above the surface of the router table. **(PHOTO D)**

SPREAD GLUE in the key slots and then individually on each key as it is pushed into place.

AFTER SANDING on the stationary belt sander, rout the bottom edge with a 45-degree chamfering bit.

Make the lid

A LID CAN BE MADE FROM EITHER MATCHING or contrasting hardwood. For this box, I used a piece of spalted sycamore. The sycamore has brown streaks and lighter tones similar to the walnut used in the miter keys and the white oak used in the body of the box.

1. Rip the lid to width, and then use the crosscut sled on the tablesaw to cut it to length. **(PHOTO A)**

2. Use the tablesaw to form a rabbet around the edge so that it will fit within the sides of the box. I use an accessory fence to allow the sawblade to be buried without cutting into the side of the tablesaw fence. Fit the lid ends first and then the front and back. Raise the blade in small increments until you get to a perfect fit. **(PHOTO B)**

3. Sand the lid and sides of the box and apply Danish oil to bring the grain and color of the woods to life.

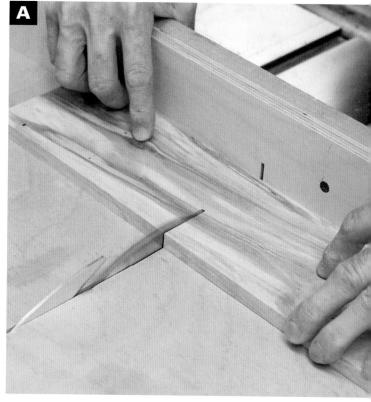

MAKE THE LID from contrasting hardwood. This one is spalted sycamore.

RABBET THE EDGES of the lid to fit the box. A notched push stick pulls the workpiece through the cut and holds it tight to the accessory fence at the same time.

Explore Shape and Keep Secrets

Altering the lines on the underside of the box offers the opportunity to add a secret compartment that becomes apparent only when the contents are removed and a lined panel is lifted out. Experimenting with line on the underside of the box also invites you to get creative with the shape, line, and focal point of the lids, too.

FORM THE BOTTOM

1. Cut the solid wood bottom from ¾-in. white oak planed to thickness. Because the bottom of this box is solid wood, it should be cut slightly narrower than would be required for a perfect fit, as it will expand and contract with changes in seasonal humidity. Cut it to a width ¹⁄₃₂ in. less than the plywood panel used in the featured box. Then, form a tongue around the bottom using the same technique used to form the tongue on the Baltic-birch plywood.
(PHOTO A)

2. Because of the additional thickness of this stock, a second step is required. Lay the stock flat on the tablesaw and with the fence set ³⁄₁₆ in. from the farthest point of the blade's cut. Set the blade height to intersect the first cuts and make the second cut. **(PHOTO B)**

TO FORM THE BOTTOM to contain the secret compartment, first make a cut along the edge with the workpiece standing against the fence.

FINISH FORMING THE TONGUE on the bottom with the stock held flat, the fence adjusted, and the blade raised to intersect the first cuts.

Box with secret compartment

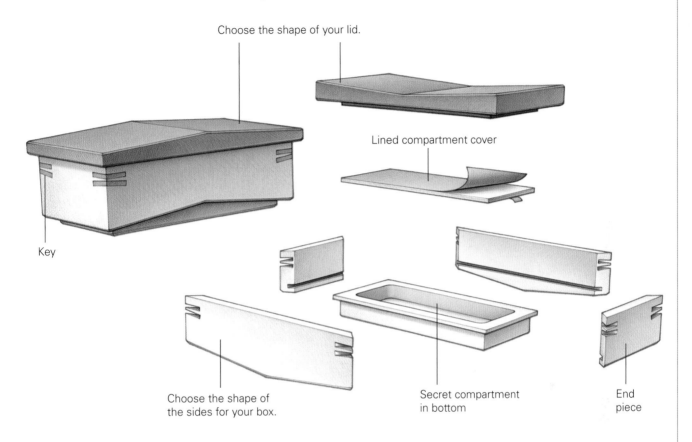

Choose the shape of your lid.

Lined compartment cover

Key

Choose the shape of
the sides for your box.

Secret compartment
in bottom

End
piece

MATERIALS

QUANTITY	PART	MATERIAL	SIZE	NOTES
2	Front and back	White oak	$\frac{3}{8}$ in. x $1\frac{7}{8}$ in. x 7 in.	
2	End pieces	White oak	$\frac{3}{8}$ in. x $1\frac{7}{8}$ in. x $3\frac{1}{2}$ in.	
1	Bottom	White oak	$\frac{3}{4}$ in. x $3\frac{11}{32}$ in. x $6\frac{5}{8}$ in.	Includes $\frac{1}{8}$-in. x $\frac{3}{16}$-in. tongue on each edge
1	Lid	Contrasting hardwood	$\frac{3}{4}$ in. x 4 in. x $7\frac{1}{2}$ in.	
8	Keys	Walnut or contrasting hardwood	$\frac{1}{8}$ in. x $\frac{5}{8}$ in. x $1\frac{1}{4}$ in.	Cut triangles from $\frac{1}{8}$-in. x $\frac{5}{8}$-in. stock.
1	Compartment cover	Baltic-birch plywood	$\frac{1}{8}$ in. x $2\frac{3}{4}$ in. x $6\frac{1}{4}$ in.	Cover with lining material

USE THE ROUTER TABLE and a ³⁄₈-in.-diameter spiral cutter to rout the inside compartment in the box base. The fence and stop blocks on three sides constrain the router cut. Raise the router in small increments.

3. Use the router table to form a recess for the secret compartment. Mount a ³⁄₈-in. spiral bit in the router table and clamp blocks around it to control the travel of the workpiece. Position stop blocks as shown in the drawing below, with the router bit at exact center. Raise the router bit in small increments between routing operations. **(PHOTO C)** Raise the router bit only ⅛ in. at a time. Forming the compartment to a depth of ⅝ in. will take five careful passes, moving the workpiece between stops.

MAKE THE FRONT, BACK, AND SIDES

1. Cut the groove to fit the box bottom ½ in. from the edge and ³⁄₁₆ in. deep. This extra distance from the edge is to allow you to shape the sides.

2. Design your box sides, remembering to keep your cuts away from the grooves cut for the bottom to fit. These lines can be straight or curved and angled toward or away from the center of the box. **(PHOTO A)**

Setup for routing inside of bottom panel

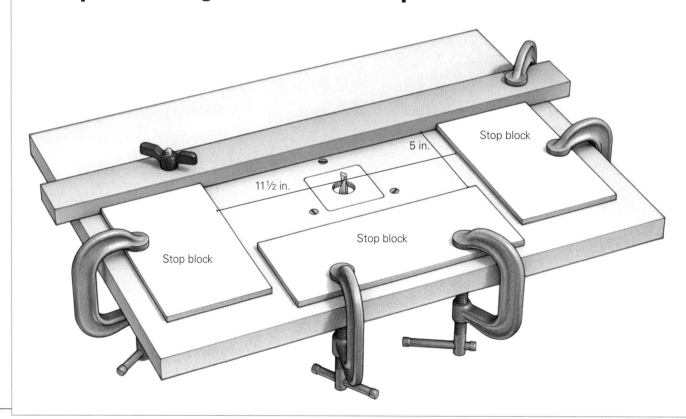

Stop block

5 in.

11½ in.

Stop block

Stop block

3. Use the bandsaw to cut the shape of the underside of the box sides. **(PHOTO B)**

4. Depending on the shape you've cut, you may choose a variety of sanding techniques to smooth the sawn surfaces. To sand those that have a recess at the center of the stock, clamp the parts together and use a sanding block and random-orbit sander to sand away the bandsaw marks. **(PHOTO C)** Take care to keep these surfaces flat.

5. For other shapes, you can use a stationary belt sander. For this shape, I taped the corners to hold them together as I sanded them, so that the ends would be sanded flush with the sides in a single operation. **(PHOTO D)**

6. Assemble the shaped sides the same way you did the featured box. Tape the corners together, apply glue, and wrap the sides around the bottom. **(PHOTO E)** But don't forget to do all necessary sanding first.

DESIGN THE EDGES of the underside of the box using pencil or pen.

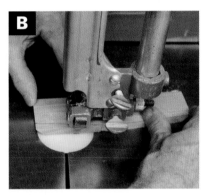

USE THE BANDSAW to cut the shape in the box front and back.

SAND CONCAVE SHAPES using sanding blocks and a random-orbit sander.

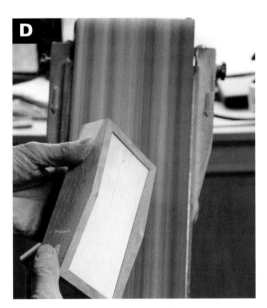

SAND FLAT SURFACES, where possible, using a stationary belt sander or flat sanding sheet.

ASSEMBLE THE BOX SIDES around the box bottom, and use rubber bands to hold things tight while glue sets.

HAVE FUN playing with lid designs.

TO MAKE A SHAPED LID I played with a variety of shapes to see what I liked best. Experimenting like this brings a sense of play into your work that others will notice and appreciate. The walnut lids shown were cut to shape using the bandsaw and then sanded, but only after the rabbet was cut to allow it to fit the finished box as shown in photo B on p. 33. You can make a domed lid using the same technique shown for making a domed panel lid starting on p. 103. **(PHOTO A)** Notice how various lid shapes interact with the lines established on the underside of the box, to create an attention-grabbing design.

1. After the box is sanded and finished with Danish oil, cut a piece of ⅛-in. Baltic birch plywood to fit inside. **(PHOTO B)** It should be loose enough to fall out but not so loose as to show gaps.

2. Glue a piece of lining material to it, trim around the edges, and attach a small lift tab of matching fabric. This will provide a cover for your secret compartment.

A SIMPLE LINED PANEL covers the secret compartment. Shhhh.

A Veneered Box

WITH THIS veneered box, we'll explore the use of color while designing a box. Color is one of the woodworker's most useful design tools, and woods from around the world, or even those in our own backyards, can come in an amazing array of colors. Those colors, whether vibrant or subdued, offer endless opportunities for choice and creativity. With color, we can create both harmony and contrast. The use of appropriate colors can help a box harmonize with its environment or make it stand out as an example of beauty and craftsmanship.

One smart way to incorporate color into your work is with veneers, which are thin-sliced pieces of wood, hardly thicker in some cases than a piece of paper. When mounted on MDF or plywood, veneers are strong enough to offer lasting beauty. With veneers, a very small amount of wood of special pattern and color can be made to stretch a very long way. Veneers are inexpensive in comparison to solid woods of the same species, so using veneers is thrifty, both for the boxmaker and for the environment.

This simple box is made with machiche, a tropical hardwood, with contrasting maple keys and a top panel veneered with lacewood. The lacewood contains many of the same color tones found in the darker machiche. The contrasting use of maple helps to accentuate the miter keys that lock the corners together. The maple lift tab also invites the user to place a finger in just the right place to open the box.

Veneered box

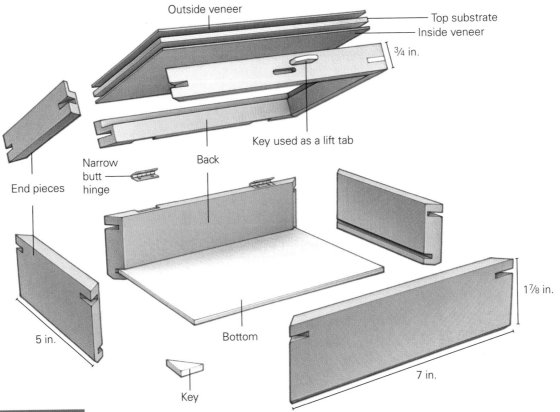

Outside veneer

Top substrate

Inside veneer

¾ in.

Key used as a lift tab

Narrow butt hinge

Back

End pieces

5 in.

Bottom

Key

1⅞ in.

7 in.

MATERIALS

QTY	PART	MATERIAL	SIZE	NOTES
2	Front and back	Machiche or other hardwood	⅜ in. x 2¾ in. x 7 in.	
2	End pieces	Machiche or other hardwood	⅜ in. x 2¾ in. x 5 in.	
1	Bottom	Baltic-birch plywood	⅛ in. x 4⅝ in. x 6⅝ in.	Check fit at trial assembly and cut smaller if necessary.
1	Outside veneer rough dimension	Contrasting hardwood	5 in. x 7 in.	Cut to fit after box is ready for assembly and substrate is veneered on both sides.
1	Top substrate	Baltic-birch plywood	⅛ in. x 5 in. x 7 in.	Cut to fit after box is ready for assembly and substrate is veneered on both sides.
1	Inside veneer rough dimension	Contrasting hardwood	5 in. x 7 in.	Cut to fit after box is ready for assembly and substrate is veneered on both sides.
9	Keys	Contrasting hardwood	⅛ in. x ⅝ in. x 1¼ in.	Cut triangles from ⅛-in. x ⅝-in. stock. (1 for lift tab)
1 pair	Hinges (narrow butt)	Brass	¾ in. x ⅝ in. open	Ace® Hardware stock number 1421 or equivalent
1	Ball chain lid support	3-in. number 3 ball chain and connectors		LeeValley.com stock number 00G48.01 for 6 sets

Color

WHEN I FIRST BEGAN WORKING WITH WOOD, I became intrigued with the variety of local hardwoods and the diverse colors and patterns of grain they presented. I began making inlay from my local Arkansas hardwoods as a way to illustrate the diversity and harmony of our local forest growth. Playing with this juxtaposition of colors, one alongside another, I gained a sense of what woods look good together. But sometimes the mixing of colors works well in a box, and sometimes the results are not as pleasing. I've been asked by my students how to mix and match colors and species of wood, and over the years I've come up with some simple guidelines that can help a beginning boxmaker to be more comfortable in the use of color.

Using dark and light woods can provide contrast to create an attention-getting box, while using woods of similar intensity and hue can bring a sense of unity and harmony to a box. Deciding whether you want to make a bold-statement box that demands attention or whether you have a more subtle purpose for making your box may help you to choose the colors of your wood. So it is important to first examine your goals. Keep in mind that bold statements are risky and you may find some advantage in being somewhat cautious in your use of color, particularly if you are just beginning your box-making adventure.

One thing you will discover in an examination of wood is that wood grain is not one consistent color. It consists of bands of light and dark and of subtle differences in hue. A single species of wood will have darker lines of grain; use woods of that darker color for accent or to provide contrast. For example, the dark grain lines in white oak are nearly the same hue as the background color of walnut. Take your cue from what you find in the grain, and your use of contrasting wood won't be far off the mark.

I've found that it is important to have a good reason for your use of color. It's more effective when it has a clear purpose. For example, the use of contrasting keys to reinforce miter joints gently reminds the viewer that the box was deliberately crafted to last for generations by a craftsman who cared about his or her work. Careful placement of those contrasting keys can create a sense of rhythm and visual balance in the design of a box. A thin line of contrasting wood can highlight and frame a panel of figured hardwood accentuating that wood. And just as a frame may be used to bring a painting to life, the body of a box done in one color of wood may highlight a more figured, colorful, and attractive lid. Contrasting colors can also serve a purpose beyond aesthetics; a small lift tab of a contrasting color directs the viewer where to open the box.

Have simple, clear design objectives for your use of colors in a box and those colors will work to make your box beautiful.

COLOR IN BOXMAKING can come from either the wood itself or from an applied finish. In this example, there are two layers of milk paint on textured wood with one color sanded through to reveal the other.

Resaw and plane the materials flat

1. Use the tablesaw or bandsaw to resaw thicker stock. If you use the tablesaw, the safest technique is to keep the blade low and cut only halfway through the stock.

2. Flip the wood end for end, keeping the same side against the fence, and finish the cut. **(PHOTO A)** Then plane the wood to its final thickness; ⅜ in. thick is ideal for making the sides of this box, but slightly thicker or thinner will not have more than a minor effect.

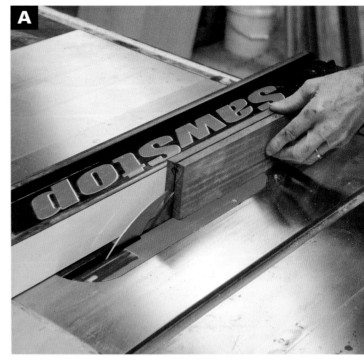

USE THE TABLESAW (or bandsaw) to resaw stock for the box sides. Keep the tablesaw blade set at just barely above half the thickness of the stock.

Miter the corners

AS WHEN MAKING THE BOX IN THE PREVIOUS chapter, begin by cutting a spacer block. For this box make a spacer 2 in. long. I will discuss proportion in greater detail on p. 92, but there is no easier way to make a box with matching grain in the corners than by using a spacer block to alternate the lengths of cut. And as you will learn in the sidebar on p. 92, there is particular magic in the 2-in. block.

1. Mark and sequentially number the parts either before or after they are cut. As with the lift-lid box (see p. 24), the first cut is made on each part outside face down. Cut the long parts with the end against the stop block and the matching short parts with the end against the spacer, which will in turn rest against the stop block.

USE THE MITER SLED on the tablesaw to cut the corners to fit. Keep the stock in order as you cut for ease of reassembly.

2. The second cut is made on each piece outside face up and with the first cut end against the stop block. This instruction applies to both left-tilt saws and right-tilt saws, the only difference being that the stop block will be clamped to the fence on the side opposite the tilt of the blade. **(PHOTO A)**

Rabbet and groove the sides for the top and bottom

AFTER THE PARTS ARE MITERED, CUT THE grooves in the sides for the bottom to fit. Use a notched push stick to apply pressure, pull the workpiece safely through the cut, and keep your hands at a safe distance from the blade. **(PHOTO A)**

Forming the rabbet on the top edge of each piece can easily be done on the router table or the tablesaw. On the router table, use a large-diameter straight-cut router bit, buried in the fence with only ¼ in. protruding. Raise the height of the router bit enough to equal the thickness of the Baltic-birch plywood top plus the thickness of the veneers to be used. **(PHOTO B)** It is better to go just a bit deeper than absolutely necessary so that when the box is assembled with the top panel in place, a bit of edge

WORK SMART

While some woodworkers cut the groove and rabbet prior to mitering the ends of each piece, I find cutting rabbets and miters on short stock increases the accuracy of each cut.

remains to be sanded down flush to the veneer rather than the other way around.

This same step can be done on the tablesaw in the following manner: Set the blade height to equal the thickness of the Baltic-birch plywood top plus the two thicknesses of veneer, and set the fence so that the distance to the outside of the cut is ¼ in. Pass the workpieces through the cut with the top edges of their face sides against the fence. Then lower the blade height to ¼ in. and, with the inside faces of each part down, make second cuts to form the rabbets. You will need to set the fence so that the distance between it and the outside of the cut equals the thickness of the Baltic-birch plywood plus the thicknesses of the veneer.

A

USE THE TABLESAW to cut grooves in the sides for the bottom panel to fit. Cut ³/₁₆ in. deep.

B

RABBET THE TOP inside edge of each side using a straight-cut bit in the router table. Use a push stick to control the stock through the cut.

When installing veneered surfaces flush to surrounding wood, leave the surrounding wood slightly proud to minimize sanding on the veneer which could lead to sanding through the veneer.

SPREAD GLUE on the Baltic-birch plywood panel for the top.

Veneer the top panel

VACUUM VENEERING USED TO BE MORE OF a professional technique, out of the reach of many amateur woodworkers due to the cost of equipment. These days, simple vacuum kits designed for making skateboards can also be used for making boxes; for example, the Roarockit vacuum veneer kit can allow you to get started for much less expense than a professional kit.

1. The veneer and plywood top panel should be ¼ in. to ⅜ in. oversize in both directions to allow it to be trimmed perfectly to fit just prior to assembly. Apply glue to the Baltic-birch plywood. **(PHOTO A)**

2. Apply veneer to both sides at the same time. Then press the veneer in place. **(PHOTO B)**

PRESS THE VENEER firmly in place. Wax paper can help to keep from getting glue where you don't want it.

3. Seal the vacuum bag and use the pump to remove the air from the bag. An expanded plastic mesh helps to provide passage for the air to be pulled from the surface of the veneer. **(PHOTO C)**

4. Leave the panel in the bag for about 45 minutes for the glue to dry. I check frequently during those minutes to see that the vacuum has held. You can tell by attempting to pump more air from the bag. If the pump operates easily, air is leaking into the bag and you must pump again to maintain clamping pressure.

USE A VACUUM PRESS to press the veneer in place. This is a simple, low-cost approach using a kit designed for skateboards, but great for boxes.

Cut the top panel to size

MEASURE INSIDE THE OPENING of the trial-assembled box to determine the size to cut the veneered top panel.

1. After the glue has set, cut the veneered top panel to size. To determine the proper size and get the best possible fit, tape the sides of the box together at the corners with masking tape, and then apply rubber bands to hold the box tight as you measure the space available in the rabbet for the veneered panel. **(PHOTO A)**

2. Your first cut along one edge of the veneered panel will align the veneers with one long edge of the Baltic-birch substrate. This will give you the first flat edge along one side. From there, cut one end square and then the other using the stop block to control the exact length. **(PHOTO B)** My preference in making this box is to set the stop block slightly too far from the cut, so that I can work my way to a perfect fit.

3. Reset the stop block location on the sled and, with one square corner held tightly to the sled and against the stop block, cut the final side to finished width. Again, it works best to start wide and work your way to a perfect cut, checking to see that it fits neatly into the top of your trial-assembled box.

USE THE 90-DEGREE CROSSCUT SLED on the tablesaw to cut the veneered panel to fit.

Assemble the box

APPLY GLUE to the miters (each side) and a bit of glue in the grooves cut for the bottom. I have three corners taped together to keep them in order and for ease of assembly.

1. Remove the rubber bands and open the box up to apply glue to the corners. Because this box is made with a Baltic-birch plywood bottom panel, you can also apply a bit of glue in the grooves at each end of each part so that the bottom will help to provide strength to the corner joints. **(PHOTO A)**

2. Roll the box sides around the bottom panel and apply rubber bands to hold the corners tight. Be prepared with additional clamps. The clamps that work best for mitered corner boxes are those that pull evenly from all four corners of the box at the same time. The picture-frame clamps shown in the top photo on the facing page are ideal. But have

B

USE A COMBINATION OF RUBBER BANDS and clamps to hold the corners tight. Then apply glue to the inside of the rabbet before pressing the veneered top panel in place.

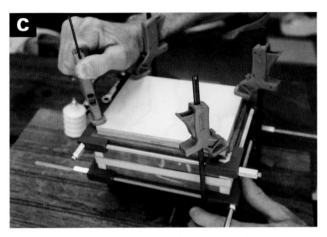

C

USE A BLOCK of wood to distribute clamping pressure as you glue the top panel in place.

them set up almost to size before you apply glue so that no time will be wasted before the glue sets. Other clamping options are shown in the sidebar on p. 48.

3. When the sides are glued tightly together, spread a bead of glue in the rabbet and press the veneered top panel into position. **(PHOTO B)**

4. Use small clamps and a plywood or particle-board caul to hold the top panel tightly in place as the glue sets. **(PHOTO C)** Make the caul only slightly smaller than the veneered panel so that it applies pressure and holds the panel flat as clamping pressure is applied at the corners.

WORK SMART

During glue-up, apply a coat of paste wax to the bottom of your caul to keep it from sticking in case extra glue seeps out. An alternate technique is to put wax paper between the caul and top panel.

Cut the miter key slots

WE ALREADY MADE A SIMPLE JIG FOR cutting the miter key slots on p. 30. Because of the depth of this box, I've chosen a different jig that gives greater support for guiding the box across the tablesaw to cut the slots.

1. The jig we are using (see p. 49) holds the box at a 45-degree angle as it passes over the saw just like the jig shown in the last chapter, but this one allows for the key slots to be cut at any position along the full height of the box. Filler pieces of

A

USE A KEYED MITER SLED to carry the box across the tablesaw to cut slots at the corners for the keys. Use a spacer block to control the position of the box on the sled.

various lengths cut to fit in the space between the box and the slide portion of the jig allow the box to be positioned exactly where you want for each cut. **(PHOTO A)**

Clamping mitered corners requires a strategy that's different from that used for other common woodworking joints. As you apply pressure from a clamp on one side of a box made with mitered corners, it forces the miter to slide in the direction pressure is applied, forcing the corners out of alignment. Mitered corners need pressure applied equally from all four corners at the same time. A variety of clamp types are designed to do this. Band clamps and picture-frame clamps pull joints together evenly, ensuring that the corners are perfectly aligned at the points of the miters.

I often use even simpler techniques. Large rubber bands or package tape are each capable of applying enough pressure to hold a well-cut mitered joint together long enough for the glue to dry. You can add as many layers of

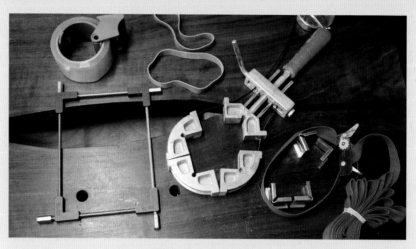

A VARIETY OF CLAMPING TOOLS work well for mitered corners. Clockwise from left: picture-frame clamp, clear tape, rubber bands, and band clamps.

tape or as many rubber bands as needed to pull the joints tight. As important as applying sufficient clamping pressure is the woodworker's careful observation of each corner before the box is set aside for the glue to dry. Using clear tape will help you to

see what you've done. Check for miters that meet very precisely at the corners and that close tight at both the top and bottom of the box. Once the glue has set, it is too late to make adjustments.

INSTALL AND GLUE all the keys in place.

2. To figure out how long to make the spacer blocks, make your first cut into the body of the jig and then measure the distance from the slide portion of the jig to the saw's cut in the "V." For my saw, that distance is about 5 in., so if I mark the desired location of my key on the box and align the 5-in. mark of my steel ruler or tape measure on that key, and subtract what remains from the top of the box to the end of the rule, I've determined how long to cut the first block. For a second or third key, I do the same thing.

3. Spread glue inside the grooves and a bit on each key as you put them in place at the corners of the box. **(PHOTO B)**

Over the years, I've made many versions of this sled and I've continually refined my design. I like this version because it is not only easy to use but also very simple to make.

Form the cradle from two pieces of ¾-in. plywood or MDF, one 5 in. wide by 9 in. long and the other 4¼ in. wide by 9 in long. Use clear plastic tape and glue to hold the two parts together to form a 90-degree angle with the edges carefully aligned. When the glue has set, make a trimming cut with the saw set at 45 degrees to form a flat edge that will allow the two parts to stand up on the tablesaw without falling. Then use a pin or brad nailer to drive nails into the joint, being careful not to put them near the area where the blade will cut.

Make the slider from a piece of hardwood planed to fit into the miter gauge slots on the top of your tablesaw. Getting just the right fit is important. It should slide without force, but not be loose enough to wiggle. While the dimensions of these parts are not critical to the use of the jig, I make mine from stock about 3½ in. wide and 15 in. long for smooth travel.

To assemble, place the slider into the miter gauge slot on the right side of the saw and clamp the cradle to it as it rests squarely on the flat surface. Then use the brad nailer to connect the slider to the "V"-shaped cradle.

USE A BRAD or pin nailer to strengthen the cradle joint after the glue sets.

DRIVE BRADS OR pins through the slider into the "V"-shaped body of the jig.

Miter key sled

9 in.

15 in.

¾ in.

4¼ in.

5 in.

Cradle

Slider

¾ in.

Flat edge

4. Sand the flat sides of the box on a belt sander. **(PHOTO C)** I turn the box end for end as I work, keeping it in one place for only a very short time, so that I can continually monitor my results and avoid sanding too heavily in one spot.

THE TRIANGULAR KEYS (as made on p. 31) can be quickly sanded flush to the surrounding sides. Use a stationary belt sander or, as a simple alternative, a sanding block or coarse sandpaper taped to the workbench.

C

Cut the lid from the body of the box

A

USE A TABLESAW to cut the lid from the body of the box.

B

TEST WITH A KNIFE after your first cut. There should be just a small amount of resistance, indicating that there is enough structure remaining to allow the box to be cut without the lid becoming loose and pressing in on the blade. Then use the knife to finish the cut and remove the lid from the body of the box.

1. Use the tablesaw to cut the lid from the body of the box. Keep the blade height low so that it does not pass all the way through the stock. **(PHOTO A)**

2. I have a knife at the ready to check my first cut. The knife should pass through the remaining stock with only a small amount of effort. **(PHOTO B)** After all the sides are cut on the tablesaw use the knife to finish the cut.

3. After the lid is cut free of the sides, place it on a large sheet of sandpaper and smooth the cut. **(PHOTO C)**

USE A SHEET OF SANDPAPER on top of the workbench to sand the edges of the lid and body of the box flush.

Install the hinges

MAKE A STORY STICK the exact length of the back edge of the box. I used ⅛-in.-thick maple stock left over from making miter keys.

I USE A SIMPLE STORY-STICK TECHNIQUE for routing mortises for butt hinges on the router table. This is a technique I've taught woodworkers in classes throughout the United States, and while it may seem a bit complicated at first, it really simplifies getting an exact fit.

1. Make a story stick of thin wood cut to the exact same length as the back edge of the box. Use your sense of touch as well as your eyes to compare and make certain that it is the same length. **(PHOTO A)** Any variance in length will lead to either a bit of extra chiseling or a gap.

2. Cut a slot in the edge of the story stick using the crosscut sled on the tablesaw. Hold the stick on edge against the fence and set the blade so that it cuts only part way through; widen the slot with more cuts until it holds the hinge just so. **(PHOTO B)** On this box, I set the hinge at 1 in. from the end of the story stick, but on wider or

USE THE SLED on the tablesaw to trim away just enough of the story stick for the hinge to fit without falling out.

narrower boxes the distance can be changed as necessary. In a perfect fit, the hinge will hang in the slot as shown on p. 51 but slide in easily without force.

3. Install a zero-clearance router table insert to help set up the height and fence position for the router table cut. With a ⅛-in. spiral router bit in the router table, raise the height to equal just less than half the thickness of the hinge. **(PHOTO C)** Then set the fence so that the hinge will fit into the mortise with at least half the barrel of the hinge protruding. The exact amount of inset of the hinge is also related to other factors like the thickness of the stock used. In all cases, butt hinges are easier to install accurately if three sides are confined within the mortise.

4. Use the story stick to set up stop blocks, left and right. I use a spiral bit that makes aligning the story stick with the full width of cut easy. If you use a router bit with straight flutes, make certain that the flutes are aligned to their widest points against the stick. Move the stick as far as it can go to the right to set up the right stop block, and then to the left to set up the left block. **(PHOTO D)**

5. Lower the top or bottom of the box onto the router table and move the back edge along the fence to rout the space on the edge for the hinge to fit. Then do the other part, being certain in each case that the back surface of the box is against the fence.

6. You will notice that this first operation will rout only one hinge mortise of each part **(PHOTO E)**. In order to rout the matching mortises, remove the stop blocks and flip the story stick to orient the other direction along the fence. Follow the same sequence to rout the matching hinge mortises in the top and bottom.

FIRST, SET UP the height of the cut and the distance of the fence to the router bit. Bit height should equal just less than half the thickness of the hinge.

SET STOP BLOCKS left and right to control the travel of the box lid and body on the router table.

ROUT WITH THE INSIDE EDGE of the box lid and then the body against the router table fence. The back surface of each part should rest on the top of the router table to get this result. Flip the story stick end for end and change the stop blocks to make the matching cuts.

Rout to fit the lift tab

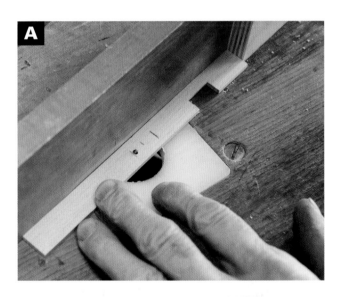

YOU'RE NOT DONE YET WITH THE STORY stick; it can still be used to fit the lift tab at the exact center of the front of the lid.

1. Align the stop block on the right to position the left side of the tab, and lower it onto the spinning router until it cuts through. **(PHOTO A)**

2. After the router is turned off and stops, flip the story stick over with the same side against the fence to position the stop block on the left. This setup, with two stop blocks, left and right, will enable you to rout a precisely centered groove to fit your lift tab. **(PHOTO B)**

(ABOVE) USE THE SAME STORY STICK to rout the groove for the lift tab. Set the stop block on the left, and then lower the stick so that the router bit bores through. Then flip the stick to set the other stop block.

(LEFT) HOLD THE INSIDE SURFACE of the box lid tight to the surface of the fence as you lower it in place and slide it back and forth between stops to rout the finger tab groove.

Cutting the tab

1. Making a tiny lift tab takes some rather close cutting with the saw. Use the eraser end of a pencil to hold down a piece of ⅛-in.-thick maple as you cut it to length to fit the groove in the front of the box. **(PHOTO C)** I use a stop block on the crosscut sled to control the length of the cut. I used a left-over miter key for this as it was already the right thickness to fit the groove. As an alternate approach, this cut can be made easily and accurately with a fine-toothed handsaw.

2. To shape the edges of the tab to fit the groove drag it along on a sheet of sandpaper as you gradually raise the angle and round it to fit. Surprisingly, this takes only a few strokes on each edge. After fitting it to the length of the groove, continue to sand on the front edges to achieve a pleasing shape. Moving gradually from coarse to fine sandpaper will give the best results. Once shaped, glue the lift tab into the slot. **(PHOTO D)**

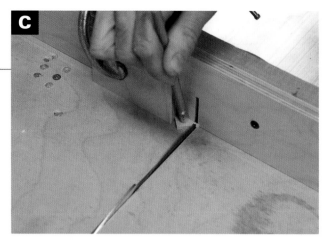

MAKING A TINY LIFT TAB takes some rather close work. Cut the tab from an extra miter key. Set the stop block on the sled and use the eraser end of a pencil to hold it tight as you make the cut.

PUT JUST A DAB OF GLUE in the slot before you glue the lift tab in place.

Install the hinges and hardware

TINY BUTT HINGES LIKE THESE ARE difficult to install. First, the screw holes must be accurately located in order to nest the hinges tightly into their mortises to guarantee that the edges of the box will be aligned. Second, tiny screws are difficult to drive into hardwood and must be predrilled.

1. I make simple drilling guides like the one shown in the top right photo on the facing page in order to simplify the exact drilling of pilot holes for the screws to get proper hinge placement. **(PHOTO A)** The great thing about making this

WORK SMART

When making a guide for drilling screw holes, use the drill press and fence for greater accuracy when drilling the guide holes.

MAKE A GUIDE block for drilling holes for the hinges to fit. Size the block to the width of the mortise and then use a drill press and fence to make certain that the pilot holes are properly located and parallel to the edge.

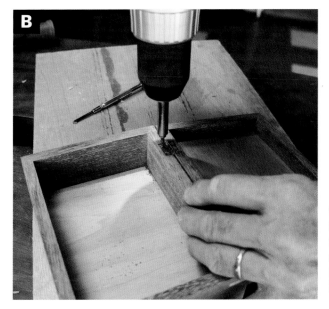

WAX THE SCREWS and, if using a power drill to drive them into place, set the clutch at the lowest setting. Nothing is worse at this point than a broken screw.

small drilling jig is that I can mess up the making of it without messing up the box.

2. After drilling the pilot holes, drive the screws in place. The screws that came with the brass hinges used with this box are brass-plated steel, and a power drill can be used to drive them in place. The clutch on the drill that allows it to slip as the screw tightens should be set at the lowest level. I install the screws in the lid first and then hold the lid in place as I drive the screws into the body of the box. **(PHOTO B)**

Screw threads should be waxed to ease their passage into hardwood. Some woodworkers use a steel screw of the same size first, and then remove it to install the brass screw with less risk of it breaking.

ATTACH A BALL chain to keep the lid from opening too far.

3. One of the best ways to support a lid on a small box and keep it from falling open too far is with a beaded chain. Check the materials list on p. 40 to find a source for parts. **(PHOTO C)**

A Mix-and-Match Lid

THE USE OF COLOR IS A FORM OF PLAY FOR THE boxmaker. Instead of a single veneer on the top, play with whatever tools you have at your disposal. For the pattern shown here, I used a paper cutter to cut thin strips of wood from various species of veneer and laid them down in a mix-and-match pattern. **(PHOTO A)** After taping the pieces together, use the paper cutter to cut them again, but at a different angle. **(PHOTO B)** After offsetting the resulting parts, tape them together again and use a hole punch to remove dots. Replace those dots with dots of another species. **(PHOTO C)** Similar mix-and-match veneering techniques can be accomplished using the scrollsaw.

(ABOVE) ASSEMBLE PATTERNS OF VENEER for a more colorful look. Alternate contrasting colors to draw greater attention to your box.

(RIGHT) MAKE ADDITIONAL CUTS using a paper cutter so that the first assembly of pieces can be further arranged into an interesting pattern.

USE A PAPER PUNCH to remove and replace dots of contrasting veneers.

Add Accents and Borders

YOU CAN ALSO ADD A BIT OF ADDITIONAL color and contrast to the top of a box by inserting a thin line of contrasting solid wood around the veneered panel in the top. For the box shown below, I cut the top panel slightly smaller and assembled thin strips of maple to fill the spaces. The strips were inserted during assembly and at the same time the panel was glued into the rabbet formed in the box sides. The maple creates greater contrast and a clear dividing line between the two distinct species of wood used for the top veneer and sides. **(PHOTO A)**

FOR A MORE REFINED LOOK, cut the top panel a bit smaller prior to assembly and insert a simple band of contrasting wood before clamping the top panel in place.

TO CREATE A BORDER AROUND a field of interesting veneer, use the vacuum veneer press to laminate thin strips of various woods into a block of wood. Simply apply glue between layers, and then wrap the edges with tape to keep them from sliding as pressure is applied. **(PHOTO A)** Use the tablesaw to cut the laminated blocks of wood into strips equal in thickness to the veneer. Note that this cut is made with the strips falling on the outside of the blade. I use a push stick to carry the tail end of the block through the saw, and have

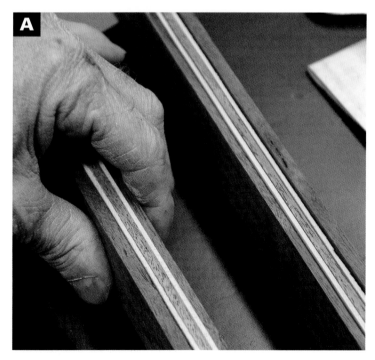

ADD A COLORFUL BORDER by assembling thin strips of wood and gluing them together in the vacuum press.

CUT THE ASSEMBLED BLOCK of wood into thin strips on the tablesaw. Have your push stick handy to finish the cut.

to adjust the fence for each cut. **(PHOTO B)** On the back side, use tape to pull the strips tightly into place surrounding the field of veneer. **(PHOTO C)** In order to glue an assembled field of veneer on the top of a box, first the lid must be cut from the base and the empty space inside the lid must be filled

with blocking of some type to keep the vacuum from crushing or distorting the lid. I use plywood blocks cut only slightly smaller than the inside of the lid, and just thick enough so that the space is completely filled. **(PHOTO D)**

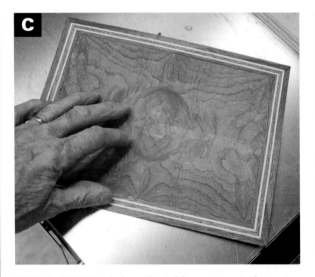

USE A MITER sled on the tablesaw to cut pieces to match around a field of colorful veneer. Use tape to secure the strips to the field of veneer thus preparing it for gluing to the lid of the box.

THE FINISHED BOX is bold and beautiful.

A Jewelry Presentation Box

O NE OF THE IMPOR-
tant principles of design,
particularly in painting or
drawing, is visual illusion in which
a two-dimensional illustration on
paper or canvas creates an image
or illusion of something that's not
really there. Lines on paper are in
fact little more than lines on paper,
but in them we may recognize
a person or a tree, and the quality of that representation is part
of our assessment of the work.
In 3-D design, the maker's objective is most often not to present
some form of illusion but rather to
offer surprise. *Effective surprise*
is a term devised by educational
psychologist Jerome Bruner to suggest that those things that surprise
us have a greater and more lasting effect. The object of good 3-D
design should be to surprise viewers in ways that incite curiosity and
lead them into closer engagement
with the object.

In order to explore how to use
effective surprise, we'll make a
jewelry presentation box. This
box is inspired by one created by

a student of mine, Alfred, who at
the age of 92 wanted to make a
small box as a gift for his wife to
celebrate their 60th wedding anni-
versary. He planned to put a pair of
diamond earrings inside.

I'll show you ways that the
inside of this box can be fitted out
for either wedding bands (if you
are planning your marriage)
or earrings (if you are in Alfred's
situation), and in either case cele-
brating a lasting relationship.

Finger-jointed ring box

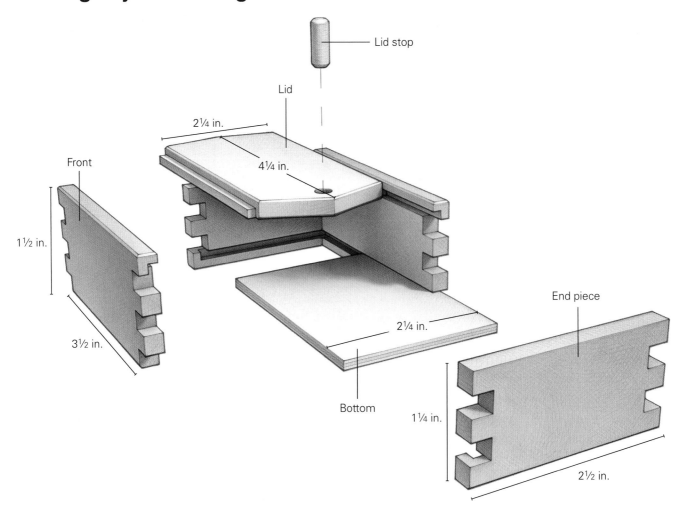

Lid stop

Lid

2¼ in.

4¼ in.

Front

1½ in.

3½ in.

Bottom

2¼ in.

End piece

1¼ in.

2½ in.

MATERIALS

QUANTITY	PART	MATERIAL	SIZE	NOTES
2	Front and back	Walnut	¼ in. x 1½ in. x 3⁹⁄₁₆ in.*	
2	End pieces	Walnut	¼ in. x 1¼ in. x 2⁹⁄₁₆ in.*	Trim to height for lid clearance.
1	Bottom	Baltic-birch plywood	⅛ in. x 2¼ in. x 3¼ in.	
1	Lid	Contrasting hardwood	¼ in. x 2⁷⁄₁₆ in. x 4¼ in.	
1	Lid stop	Hardwood dowel	¼ in. x ⅝ in.	Taper the ends with sandpaper.

*length includes ¹⁄₁₆-in. sanding allowance.

Effective Surprise

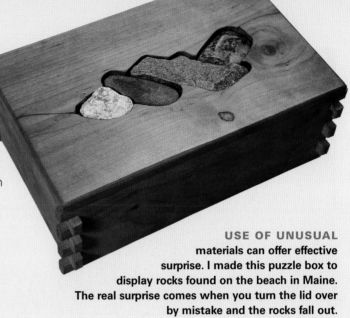

USE OF UNUSUAL materials can offer effective surprise. I made this puzzle box to display rocks found on the beach in Maine. The real surprise comes when you turn the lid over by mistake and the rocks fall out.

RESEARCHERS AND PSYCHOLOGISTS HAVE shown that parts of the brain increase in activity when the mind is challenged by surprises. Through surprise, the whole body can be called into a state of alert in which memory, learning, and depth of engagement are greatly enhanced. In two-dimensional art, one of the design objectives is "visual illusion," in which the artist creates an artificial scene by hand, brush, and paint, designed to engage the viewer. The maker of a 3-D object has similar goals. Just as the reality of a painted scene may draw the viewer in deeper, the element of surprise draws the viewer of a box to look more closely at it, reach for it, and discover its fine craftsmanship. Surprise has a physiological effect that artists and craftsmen use to their advantage in order to create both beautiful and engaging works.

One of the biggest challenges for a boxmaker is to deliver surprise in a finished box. These days with books, magazines, and the Internet, it is easy to think you've seen everything and wonder how to come up with anything fresh and new.

But "effective" surprise is not just a matter of being "different." Simply trying to be different without other purpose often leads to ineffective results like poor craftsmanship, a box that's less than useful, or a box that won't last. Even worse is that overly contrived differences—those having no other purpose—may ultimately bore the viewer.

Irish poet and social critic Oscar Wilde once said, "I have found that all ugly things are made by those who strive to make something beautiful, and that all beautiful things are made by those who strive to make something useful." While I do not agree with Wilde completely, and do find beauty in many "useless" things, the challenge of effective surprise asks that we corral our efforts to surprise within effective guidelines.

And so, what are those guidelines? First, simply choose to create useful and lasting beauty in your boxes. Because beautiful natural materials are becoming harder to find, trust your use of those materials to create surprise. The spalted maple used in the lid of the box in this chapter offers unique beauty. In an age in which most things are made by machines, the level of your craftsmanship will also create a sense of surprise in your finished box. Miter keys, doweled miter joints, hidden splines revealed only when a box is opened, finger joints, and dovetails all convey a sense that a craftsman was present and attentive during the making of a box. Also, remember that form follows function, and that if a box is useless, or difficult to use, it may fall into disfavor. How a box is used, how a lid opens, or the specific purpose for which the box was created may impart a sense of playfulness or deeper meaning. And remember that very small differences in how a box is made, no matter how subtle, can be surprising.

Learn the basics of quality work. Let a beautiful piece of wood, a new technique promising greater beauty and longevity, or a loving relationship inspire you. Attempt to make your work useful. Then, with a spirit of playfulness and creativity, make boxes.

USE THE CROSSCUT sled (as shown on p. 25) on the tablesaw to cut the front, back, and ends to length. Adjust the stop block to cut the appropriate lengths.

Prepare the stock

FIRST, MILL YOUR STOCK TO DIMENSION.
For this box, the front, back, and ends can be as thin as ¼ in., and if you are following the materials list on p. 60, the more accurately you plane your stock to this dimension, the better your parts will fit. My student Alfred and I each chose walnut for making this box, but any hardwood can be used. The box can also be altered in size to present other items of jewelry.

Cut the parts to size

USE THE CROSSCUT SLED ON THE TABLE-
saw to cut the parts to length. **(PHOTO A)** I cut mine ¹⁄₁₆ in. longer than is listed in the materials list so that there will be just a bit of length in the finger joints to be sanded flush after the box is glued and assembled. Use a pencil to hold the stock tightly against the stop block during this cut to make certain it is under control through the cut.

Finger-joint router table

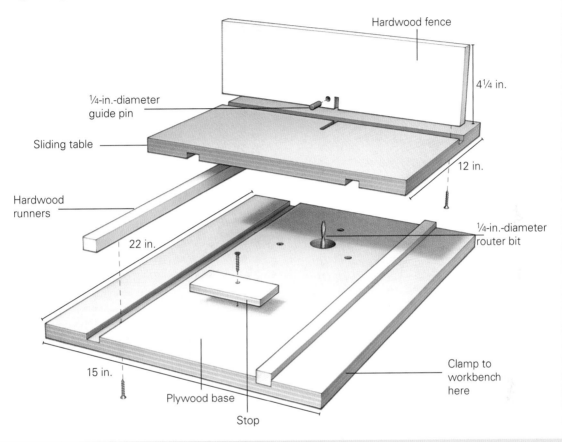

Hardwood fence

4¼ in.

¼-in.-diameter
guide pin

Sliding table

12 in.

Hardwood
runners

¼-in.-diameter
router bit

22 in.

Clamp to
workbench
here

15 in.

Plywood base

Stop

QUANTITY	PART	MATERIAL	SIZE	NOTES
1	Base	Plywood or MDF	¾ in. x 15 in. x 22 in.	
1	Sliding table	Plywood or MDF	¾ in. x 12 in. x 15 in.	
2	Runners	Hardwood	⅝ in. x ¾ in. x 22 in.	
1	Fence	Hardwood	¾ in. x 4¼ in. x 15 in.	
1	Guide pin	Steel	¼ in. diameter	An old router bit shaft will do.
6	Screws	Steel	#6 x 1 in.	Additional 1-in. machine screws will be necessary to mount the router base.
1	Stop	Hardwood	¼ in. x 2 in. x 3 in.	

I made this dedicated finger-joint router table to allow me to go directly from cutting parts to size at the tablesaw to joining them at the corners without going through any further setup. Woodworkers have many options for making this joint, from shopmade jigs and fixtures for the tablesaw or router table to professionally made jigs from your favorite wood-working tool supplier. But there is a special satisfaction in making things for yourself.

CUT THE TABLE AND SLIDER

I built my finger-joint router table using some scrap furniture-grade plywood for the base and sliding table, hard maple for the runners, and maple again for the fence. You can substitute MDF for the plywood. For the guide pin, I used a broken-off shaft from a router bit. Its ¼-in. diameter equals the width of cut of the bit used for ¼-in. finger joints.

1. After cutting the plywood parts to size, mount a ¾-in. dado blade in the tablesaw with the height set at ⅜ in. to cut dadoes for the runners halfway through the stock. I set the fence 1½ in. from the blade and cut parallel dadoes along both edges of the plywood stock. This same operation must be done to both the top and bottom plywood parts.

DRIVE SHORT SCREWS through the underside of the base into the runners to lock them in place. Drill and countersink the holes first.

2. Cut a dado of the same size and depth in the sliding table to accommodate the fence.

SIZE THE RUNNERS AND FENCE

When the dadoes have been cut, plane the runners and fence to fit. The runners should be planed to an almost tight fit, so they can slide smoothly. If they are too loose, you will lose some accuracy in use. In planing the fence to fit the dado, I prefer a snug fit, one that almost needs to be forced into place, as this fit will hold parts in relationship to each other as the final adjustments are made.

MOUNT THE ROUTER BASE AND RUNNERS

1. Mark a centerline for mounting the router base, and then drill a hole for the router collet to fit. I used a 1⅜-in. drill bit to provide adequate clearance, allowing the router collet to spin without touching.

2. Remove the base plate from the router, position it over the collet hole you just drilled, and carefully mark the location of the screw holes for mounting the router base to the table base. I simply put the router base plate in place and use a pencil to mark the screw locations.
(PHOTO A) Drill screw holes and countersink them

REMOVE THE ROUTER'S base plate and use it as your guide to mark the screw holes for attaching the router to the top side of the base. Countersink the holes drilled from this side so that the router can be attached to the other side.

from the top side. You will need longer screws to mount the base to the table than those used to secure the router base plate. I used heavier screws as well and tapped the screw holes in the router base to accommodate the larger diameter of these screws.

3. Next, drill and countersink holes for attaching the runners to the base. **(PHOTO B)**

ROUT THROUGH THE SLIDING TABLE
Clamp the router table base to the corner of a workbench and position the fence in the sliding table. You'll need to screw a stop on the plywood base to control the motion of the sliding portion of the router table. To do so, first cut into the fence so that the router bit is buried just over half its diameter. Then screw the stop onto the base so the bit can go no deeper into the fence. This prevents the router bit from gradually passing clear through the fence and putting unwary fingers at risk.

FIT THE GUIDE PIN
I use the shaft of a ¼-in. router bit as the guide pin. The round shape allows the workpiece to lift on and off the router table easily, and the guide pin can be fitted exactly by simply drilling a ¼-in. hole in the fence and pushing the pin in place. In addition, the round shape of the pin will keep small amounts of sawdust from getting in the way as you lift the parts into place.

1. Carefully measure and mark the location for the guide pin. Measure over ⅜ in. from where the router cut into the fence, and mark the location with a sharp awl, ⅛ in. above the surface of the sliding table.

2. Remove the fence from the sliding table and drill the hole. After putting the pin in place you'll be ready to make your first finger joints.

MAKE YOUR FIRST TEST CUTS
1. To prepare for making your first test cuts, raise the height of the router bit to just barely over the thickness of the stock. Then slide the first test piece over snug to the guide pin and make your first cut.

2. Step the workpiece over the guide pin for each subsequent cut.

3. When all those cuts have been made, turn the piece over from one face to the other to use it as a spacer to position the next adjoining cut as shown on p. 66. Proceed with the subsequent cuts on the matching part. Then test the fit.

ADJUST THE FIT
1. If the fingers fit together too tightly, use a hammer or mallet to tap lightly on the fence at the right side to narrow the space between the guide pin and the router cut. If the fit is too loose, tap lightly on the left. A finger placed where the edge of the fence and the edge of the sliding table align helps to gauge the amount of movement that results.

2. After making the adjustment, run another test corner to assess the fit. When you get a perfect fit, drive screws through the sliding table into the fence to lock it permanently in place.

USING YOUR FINGER-JOINT ROUTER TABLE
With this dedicated finger-joint router table, if you make a box with thick sides and then want to make one with thin sides, you may get some tearout on the back side of the cut. This is one of the most common problems whether you are cutting finger joints on the tablesaw or router. I use a piece of backing stock to refresh the backing when cutting thinner parts. Made from a piece of hardwood or plywood, this backing stock simply fits over the pin and provides fresh backing to the cut.

If you commonly make finger joints in a variety of sizes, you may also want to make sliding tables and fences for more than one bit size. The base where the router is mounted can fit more than one size of dedicated sliding table made to fit a variety of router bit sizes.

FORM ¼-IN. FINGER joints at the ends of each piece. When forming the sides, make only three cuts at each end so that you leave room for the slot that holds the sliding lid.

Form the finger joints

1. Cut the finger joints using the finger-joint router table or on the tablesaw (see the sidebar on pp. 63–65). Be careful when cutting this joint that the cuts stop short of the top on the front, back, and ends to allow for the sliding top to fit. **(PHOTO A)**

2. After the fingers are formed on the sides of the box, flip one finished part around sideways (as shown) so that the first finger can serve as a spacer for the next cuts. **(PHOTO B)**

TO POSITION AN END for its first cuts, reverse one finger-jointed box side over the guide pin to fill the space between the pin and router bit.

Rout to fit the bottom and sliding lid

A

ROUT TO FIT the bottom. Stop blocks on the router table constrain the movement of the parts so the groove will not be visible on the outside of the finished box.

B

ROUT THE GROOVE for the sliding lid panel. This operation does not require stop blocks as the groove must go all the way through the length of each part to allow the lid to slide through.

1. Use the router table with a ⅛-in. straight-cut router bit to cut the groove in the front, back, and ends for the bottom panel to fit. Use stops to limit the travel and keep the router cut from being exposed at the ends of each part. **(PHOTO A)**

2. After the grooves are cut for the bottom to fit, adjust the router fence to rout the grooves for the sliding lid. Because these grooves must be open on the ends for the sliding lid to pass, no router table stops are required. **(PHOTO B)**

Assemble the box

1. Cut the bottom panel to fit, and then sand it and all inside surfaces of the box parts before assembly, as you will not get a chance to do so after gluing.

2. I use a 45-degree chamfering router bit to relieve the top edges of the parts. The inside edges in particular must be routed before assembly.

3. Use a squeeze bottle to apply just a dab of glue on each inside surface of the finger joints and then push the parts together surrounding the bottom panel. If your finger joints are a tight fit, no clamping will be needed. If they are slightly loose, use rubber bands to hold the parts tight as the glue sets.

Fit the lid

TRIM THE BOX ends to height using the sled on the tablesaw. Making a small cut like this on small parts is easier and safer on the sled than trying to use the ripping fence.

A

1. Trim the end pieces so that the sliding lid can pass over them in both directions. Because of the short length of this part, I find it safest to use the tablesaw sled for this cut. **(PHOTO A)**

2. Cut the rabbet on the edge of the sliding lid so that it fits into the grooves cut on the box sides. **(PHOTO B)** I do this with a router table and a large straight-cut router bit. The Plexiglas® shield is clamped in place to keep my fingers safe at all times during the routing operation, and it also serves to hold the stock tight to the fence. A zero-clearance insert on the router table is required to support the stock all the way through the cut.

ROUT THE EDGES of the sliding lid using a large-diameter straight-cut router bit on the router table. The Plexiglas guide clamped to the top of the router table keeps fingers safe.

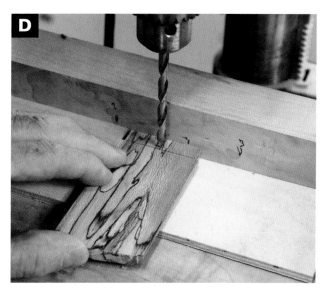

USE THE TABLESAW sled to trim the parts of the tongue on the sliding lids that would stick out when the box is closed. The blade height should be set at ⅛ in., and the stop block controls the length of the cut. Slide the stock away from the stop block while the sled brings the blade to the highest point of its cut.

DRILL A HOLE in the lid to hold a stop pin made from ¼-in. dowel stock.

3. Use the tablesaw with the blade height set at ⅛ in. to trim the edges of the tongue to match the length of the box. To do this, position the sled so that the blade is cutting at full height and then move the lid in toward the stop block. The blade will nibble away the excess length of the sliding lid tongue so it doesn't protrude beyond the edges of the box. **(PHOTO C)**

4. Drill a hole in the lid for a stop pin to fit. First, I slide the lid into position and then mark on the underside where the edge of the box stops. When using ¼-in. dowels for your stop pins as I am here, position the hole ⅛ in. from the pencil line that represents the edge of the box. Drill the hole for the ¼-in. pin using the drill press. **(PHOTO D)**

5. Use a disk sander to shape the lid as you like. **(PHOTO E)**

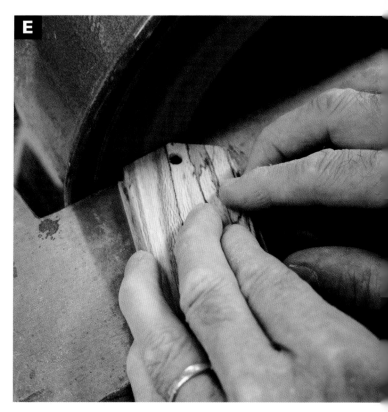

USE A DISK SANDER to shape the ends of the box lid.

Make a Mitered Variation

CUTTING A MITERED FINGER JOINT will be a new exercise for most woodworkers (one that most of my students have difficulty with), and yet it can be easily accomplished (with practice) after leaving extra width at the top of the box sides. Setting up the tablesaw to make the cut is a trial-and-error operation as the blade height and stops on a miter gauge are adjusted for a perfect fit. In order for this joint to fit, an equal amount must be cut from each side of the joint, and the cut must be precise to allow the parts to come completely together without gaps.

1. Set the height of the sawblade's cut to equal the thickness of the remaining fingers on the top edges of the box. Do not cut too deep as this will make the top fingers too loose for effective gluing. **(PHOTO A)**

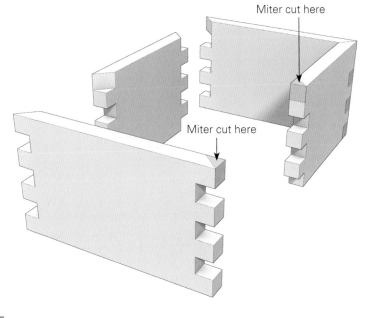

Miter cut here

Miter cut here

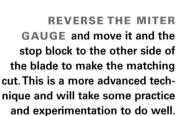

USE A MITER GAUGE with a stop block on the tablesaw to cut a mitered top edge on the finger-jointed sides and end. The blade height must be carefully set and the saw blade must be aligned to the depth of the finger-joint cuts.

2. Cut the miters at both ends of the box back and on opposite sides of the ends, leaving one end of each uncut to house the sliding lid. Change the miter gauge to the other side and also flip the fence so that the matching cuts can be made. **(PHOTO B)** The mitered finger joint requires that the tongue be formed on three sides of the sliding lid.

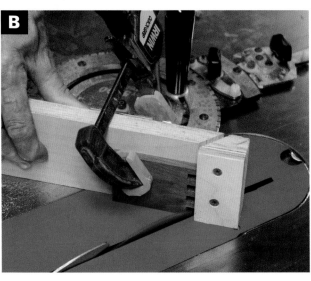

REVERSE THE MITER GAUGE and move it and the stop block to the other side of the blade to make the matching cut. This is a more advanced technique and will take some practice and experimentation to do well.

Angle the Sides

THIS BOX CAN EASILY BE MODIFIED in a variety of ways to make it even more expressive. One way is by making it from thicker stock, which allows the outside to be bandsawn to a new shape after assembly. **(PHOTO C)** Using stock that is ½ in. thick, form the finger joints and assemble the box. Then tilt the bandsaw and trim the sides as shown, leaving the sides thinner at the top and still full thickness at the bottom.

These boxes can also be made in a variety of sizes, and you can change the orientation in which the lid opens, either the long way or short. You can also vary the shape of the pull that extends beyond the sides of the box. While I chose an angular design to go with the shape of the angled sides on these boxes, you might try a curve. In any case, have fun with the design and alter it to your heart's content. **(PHOTO D)**

FOR A MORE INTERESTING LOOK, make a box with thick sides and give it additional shape using the bandsaw. The angle of the cut used here is 5 degrees. Sand the surfaces smooth after the box is cut to shape.

THESE BOXES CAN BE CRAFTED in a variety of shapes and sizes, and the lid can be oriented one way or the other to make the best use of the inside space.

Think Inside the Box

THE REAL SURPRISE OFTEN COMES WHEN the box is opened to reveal what's inside. You can make a simple ring holder with paper, glue, and builder's foam. Cut three foam blocks to nearly fill the space on the inside of the box, leaving about ⅛ in. between. **(PHOTO A)** Then, cut and fold decorative paper or fabric to fit. **(PHOTO B)** Spread glue on the foam blocks and secure the lining material. You may have to hold the parts together, using either your hands or rubber bands, for a few minutes while the glue sets. **(PHOTO C)**

To customize your box for earrings, insert a simple piece of thin wood the fits from corner to corner. This divider provides a place for the earring hooks to rest. Simple carved notches hold one earring on each side and allow each to be easily removed. **(PHOTO D)**

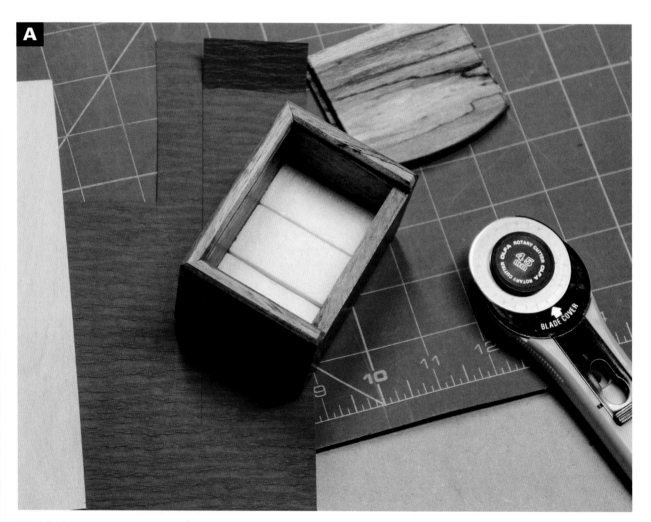

THE MOST EFFECTIVE surprise may come with what's found inside. Make a ring pillow to hold wedding bands by cutting foam blocks to fit loosely inside the box.

CUT AND FOLD decorative paper or fabric to conform to the foam blocks.

USE WOOD GLUE to attach the paper or fabric to the foam blocks. Hold or clamp the material tightly to the foam as the glue sets, being careful not to crush the foam.

FINISH THE EARRING box with small cuts to the top of the divider to give the earrings places to rest on both sides. To finish the ring box, press the ring pillow in place. Now your boxes will be ready to surprise with what's inside.

A Bracelet Box

THIS SMALL HINGED box will allow us to explore the use of rhythm in box-making. Every box can offer the opportunity to explore new designs, and one of the objectives of good design is rhythm. In fact, rhythm is both an objective of good design and also a design tool that can be applied to make a box more interesting and beautiful. This bracelet box is made with walnut and contrasting maple, and the maple offers an example of how the patterns inherent in beautiful wood can create a sense of rhythm. This particular piece of maple would be described as curly, in that the grain has a gentle, undulating visual effect.

As shown in the variations at the end of the chapter, rhythm can be established in other ways and in a more deliberate fashion than simply through the selection of wood. The use of visible keys in contrasting woods, the natural patterns left by the process of milling lumber, and texturing tools can all be used to establish rhythm. This chapter, however, can't explore all the possibilities in the use of rhythm, leaving many for you to discover on your own.

The box featured here can be used as a gift box for a bracelet or watch, but I've also made similarly sized boxes for pens and pencils and for handcrafted knives. As with other boxes in the book, it can be easily resized for a variety of other uses.

Bracelet box

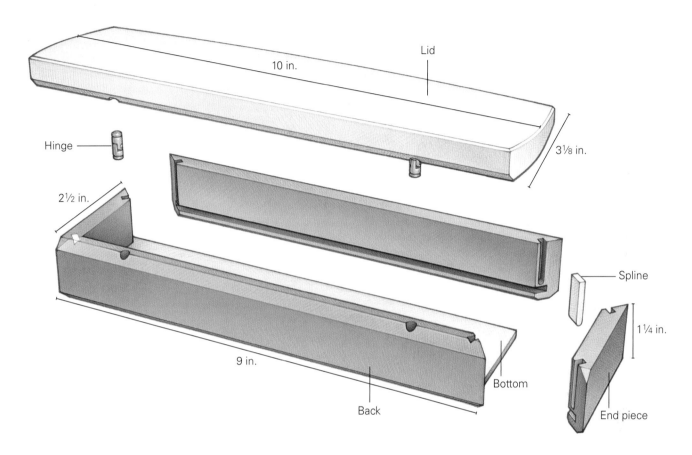

Lid

10 in.

Hinge

3⅛ in.

2½ in.

Spline

1¼ in.

9 in.

Bottom

End piece

Back

MATERIALS

QUANTITY	PART	MATERIAL	SIZE	NOTES
2	Front and back	Walnut	⅜ in. x 2⅝ in. x 9 in.	
2	End pieces	Walnut	⅜ in. x 2⅝ in. x 2½ in.	
2	Bottoms	Baltic-birch plywood	⅛ in. x 2⅛ in. x 8⅝ in.	Measure and cut to fit.
2	Lids	Contrasting hardwood	⅝ in. x 3⅛ in. x 10 in.	
8	Splines	Contrasting hardwood	⅛ in. x 2 in. x 5/16 in.	Rip to 2 in. width then cut short pieces 5/16 in. long.
2 pair	Brass hinges		5mm mini barrel hinges	www.LeeValley.com stock number 00D81.50

All materials are enough for 2 boxes.

Rhythm

RHYTHM IS AN IMPORTANT DESIGN
tool in making a beautiful wooden box.
Through the deliberate use of rhythm, a
boxmaker takes a static object and brings
it to life, inviting the eye and hand of the
viewer into direct engagement with the
box. Natural rhythm is inherent in wood
grain. The undulating fiddleback grain on
the maple lid of the lead box in this chapter (see p. 74) exhibits a visual rhythm
and movement inherent in some select
pieces of hardwood. But even without such
distinctive figure, each piece of wood has
its own rhythm found in the lines of grain
recording the growth of the tree. Paying
attention to that rhythm is much of what the box
designer does. We examine the wood, find rhythms
of order and chaos within it, and then put it to its best
use. Where rhythm is not strongly stated within the
wood itself, a boxmaker may choose to add rhythms of
his or her own.

Boxmakers have a wide array of design tools
to establish a sense of rhythm. Alternating colored
veneers on the surface of a box can establish rhythm.
When carefully placed, contrasting colored keys used
to strengthen mitered joints can also establish a sense
of rhythm and a sense of longevity. There is a sense of
rhythm in the placement of the dowels used to secure
the corners in the jewelry box on p. 118. The same can
certainly be said about the finger joints used in the
finger-jointed chest on p. 90. Their spacing offers a
precise rhythm at each corner of the box. All of these
rhythms establish that a craftsman carefully created
each beautiful work.

It has been said that every tool leaves its mark. I
find the marks of tools to be beautiful and engaging.
Just as the grain records the story of the growth of the
tree, the markings left on wood record the journey of

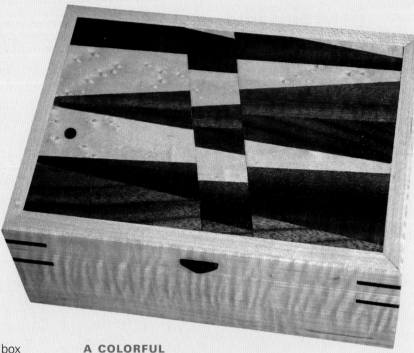

**A COLORFUL
PATTERN** moving across the surface
of a box can establish a sense of rhythm.

the material and the path of the craftsman in making
a beautiful box. For instance, the rhythmic pattern left
by the original milling of stock as it was cut from logs
to lumber is part of the story told by the wood and can
be left to engage viewers in the surface qualities and
rhythm of a wooden box. You can also impart rhythm of
your own by using various tools to create texture. For
the lid on the box variation (see p. 88), I chose to use
an almost random action to establish a chaotic pattern,
just as one might find a glimpse of chaos in the grain
of wood.

I think of rhythm as a way of establishing relation-
ships with both order and chaos within a box. Order
suggests that the box was created with deliberate con-
sciousness by a craftsman. Chaos on the other hand,
leads the viewer to connect the object with nature,
where we are used to seeing beauty in apparently
random forms and arrangements. I find boxmaking at
its best to be a balance of both.

Miter the corners

A

USE THE MITER sled, stop block, and 6½-in. spacer block to alternate between cutting the box front or back and the shorter ends.

TO SIMPLIFY THE JOINERY PROCESS IN making this box, I actually build two boxes at the same time and cut them apart after assembly.

1. After planing the material to thickness and ripping it to width, use the miter sled and stop block as shown on p. 25 to cut the front, back, and ends to length. I use a spacer block 6½ in. long between cuts, so while the first part is cut to 9 in. long, the second will be only 2½ in. long. It is very easy to change the proportions of this box simply by changing the length of the spacer block. **(PHOTO A)**

Smaller pieces can be a challenge to cut safely, so I use the eraser end of a pencil to keep the parts nested tightly against the stop block and my fingers a safe distance from the blade.

B

WITH THE SPACER block removed, as shown, cut the long parts. Then replace the spacer block and cut the last end.

2. Remove and replace the spacer block between parts and mark them as they come off the saw so that they can be arranged in order with grain matches at each corner. **(PHOTO B)**

To rout grooves to fit hidden splines I use a simple jig to guide the parts of a box across the router table. This technique provides for a very strong, but hidden joint— hidden that is until the lid is opened and your secret craftsmanship is revealed. Using this technique allows carefully matched grain to wrap undisturbed around a box's mitered corners.

A cutout on the front side of the base allows for a clamp to be more easily affixed when routing the ends of small parts. I made my jig from one piece of scrap ¾-in. plywood 8 in. wide by 12 in. long. As an alternate material try MDF.

1. Use the miter sled to cut the plywood into two parts at a 45-degree angle, and then use the bandsaw to cut away the space for a C-clamp to fit.

2. Carefully align the two parts and use tape to hold them in position. **(PHOTO A)**

3. Fold back the taped joint and apply glue. **(PHOTO B)**

4. Allow gravity and a bit of additional tape to hold the parts together as the glue sets. After 45 minutes or so, use screws, brads, or pins to strengthen the connection between the two parts. **(PHOTO C)**

5. Finally, add a guide strip to the edge of the jig to help to position the parts for routing.

USE TAPE TO ALIGN the front part of the jig to the base.

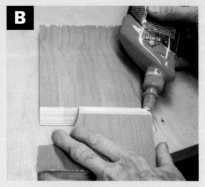

WITH THE TAPE holding the two parts, fold the base back and apply glue.

6. To use the jig, simply align the part to be routed so that its edge is perfectly flush with the bottom edge of the jig as shown in the bottom photo on p. 80. Clamp the part in place and move the body of the jig between stops on the router table.

ALLOW THE ASSEMBLED JIG to rest with the parts in position as the glue dries. Wait 45 minutes before using brads, pins, or screws to permanently position the parts.

Hidden spline jig

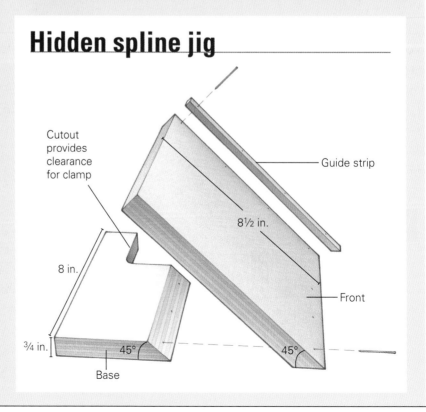

Cutout provides clearance for clamp

Guide strip

8½ in.

8 in.

Front

¾ in.

45°

45°

Base

Groove the sides to fit the bottom

1. Set the blade height at ³⁄₁₆ in. and set the fence so that there is about ³⁄₁₆ in. between the blade and fence. Then make a cut on the top and bottom inside edge of the front, back, and sides. (Remember that you're making two boxes and will cut them apart after assembly.)

USE THE TABLESAW and push stick to make grooves for the bottoms to fit. Cut both the top and bottom of each piece. This operation will make two boxes to be cut apart after assembly.

Use a push stick to guide the wood safely through the cut. **(PHOTO A)**

2. Cutting the hidden spline slots at the ends of the miters requires a special jig (as shown on the facing page) to hold the stock at a 45-degree angle as it travels over the bit in the router table. This simple, easy-to-make device allows the workpiece to be clamped tightly in place as the jig slides between stops, creating a groove for a spline to fit that is invisible on the outside of the box. Here, we are making two boxes at the same time; the wider stock offers more surface area for clamping and for riding flush with the surface of the router table. (Not only is it a nice thing to make two boxes at the same time, but it can also ease the process.)

3. Put a workpiece in the jig inside out (i.e., backward) so you can observe the relationship between the grooves and the stop and start points as the jig travels along the fence. The ⅛-in. spiral cutter should be raised to a height of about ⁵⁄₃₂ in. Adjust the stop blocks so that the groove is an equal distance from each edge and does not interfere with the grooves cut for the box bottoms. **(PHOTO B)**

4. Mounting the workpiece in the jig requires great care to make certain that the grooves are cut precisely for perfect alignment at the corners. I put the jig down on a hard, flat surface like the surface of the router table or work bench, and hold both the workpiece and the jig tight to that same surface as I put the clamp in place and apply pressure.

WITH THE ROUTER off and the workpiece reversed on the body of the jig, set the stop blocks to control the travel of the jig on the router table.

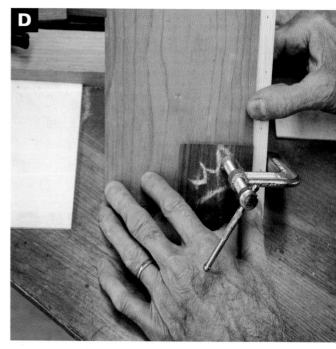

TO BEGIN THE CUT, lower the jig and workpiece over the router bit with the jig held firmly against the fence and stop block.

SLIDE THE JIG and workpiece forward and then back between stops, while holding the jig tight to the fence.

Check carefully after clamping to make certain that the edge of the workpiece and the bottom edge of the jig are perfectly flush. If they are not, the corners of the box may be misaligned.

5. With the workpiece clamped with the inside surface against the body of the jig, place the jig against the router table fence and hard against the stop block on the right, and lower it into the cut. **(PHOTO C)**

6. Move the jig from right to left and back while holding it tight against the fence. **(PHOTO D)**

The photo at right shows the finished groove. Note that it is offset toward the inside of the box, which actually centers it in the mitered joint. **(PHOTO E)**

THE FINISHED GROOVE should be spaced equally from both sides and 1/16 in. from the inside edge.

Cut the splines

1. To make the hidden splines, plane the hardwood material down to a thickness to fit. I resaw stock about ³⁄₁₆ in. thick and then pass it through the planer to get it to fit in the groove. Rip that stock so that the final width is slightly less than the length of the groove in the mitered ends of the box. This allows for discrepancies in the distance from the end of the grooves to the edge of the box. Use a ¹⁄₁₆-in.-radius roundover bit to round the edges of the hidden spline stock or simply sand the edges round with a sanding block.

CUT THE SPLINE STOCK to exact length using the crosscut sled and stop block.

2. Cut the splines to length using the crosscut sled and stop block. **(PHOTO F)** Getting the length of these splines exact is important. If they are too long, they will hold the box corners apart. If they are too short, a small gap may be visible on the inside of the box. A test fit of the spline in a box corner before assembly will help to ensure that the spines are being cut the right length and prevent problems when you are ready to glue the box together.

3. Measure the insides of the grooves cut for the bottoms to fit, and then cut the bottoms to those dimensions.

4. Sand the bottoms and the inside surfaces of the box sides before assembly as you will not be able to do these things afterwards. I also use a 45-degree chamfering bit in the router table to shape the inside edge of each part (again, this is a task that cannot be done after assembly).

Assemble the box

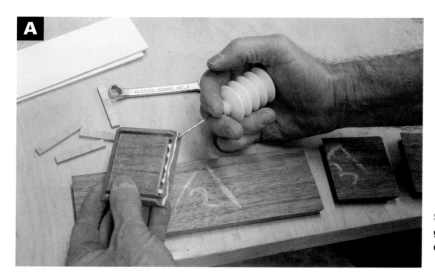

1. Use a squeeze bottle to apply glue to the insides of the spline grooves and then spread glue along the miters of each part. **(PHOTO A)**

SPREAD GLUE in the grooves and on the surface of the miter joints.

2. Put the splines in place and gradually assemble the sides around the Baltic-birch plywood box bottoms, keeping the grain matched at each corner. **(PHOTO B)**

3. While tape and rubber bands are often strong enough to clamp mitered boxes while the glue sets, my experience with the hidden spline joint is that it often takes a bit of additional force to pull the joints tight. Picture-frame clamps that pull evenly on each corner work well to hold parts tight as the glue sets. **(PHOTO C)**

CAREFULLY ASSEMBLE the sides and ends around the Baltic-birch plywood bottoms.

USE CLAMPS to pull the corners tight.

Separate the two boxes

1. After the glue sets, use the tablesaw with the blade height set just below the thickness of the stock to cut the assembled closed-form box into two boxes. **(PHOTO D)**

CUT THE TWO BOXES APART, but set the blade height for this cut so it doesn't cut all the way through the stock. This leaves a sliver of wood between the boxes to be cut with a knife. This technique keeps the box from pushing into the blade and provides a much safer cut.

2. Use a knife to finish the cut. Carefully break any remaining edge back toward the outside of the box (rather than toward the inside) as this will give a cleaner edge on the inside of the box. **(PHOTO E)** At this point, you can see the contrasting spline, providing evidence that a craftsman was present in the making of this box.

USE A KNIFE to finish the cut and then remove the remaining slivers of wood.

Make the lid

THE LID REQUIRES A BIT OF THICKNESS AT the back of the box to accommodate the type of hinge used. But that same thickness at the front of the box would make the lid heavy and thick and the design less delicate. A simple solution is to make an angled cut on the bandsaw, leaving the lid ⅝ in. thick at the back and only ⁵⁄₁₆ in. thick at the front edge. This technique, particularly when used with

additional curved cuts, leads to some interesting optical effects, giving the lid's flat planes a sense of curvature that tricks the eyes in a pleasant way.

1. Plane the wood for the lid to thickness and rip it to width. Then, with the bandsaw table tilted to about 5 degrees, make the angle cut along the length of the stock. **(PHOTO A)**

WORK SMART

When you cut your lids to length, use a stop block on the sled for precise cuts. Also cut a story stick of the exact same length to use to set up stops for drilling the holes for the mini barrel hinges.

USE THE BANDSAW to cut the sloping lid.

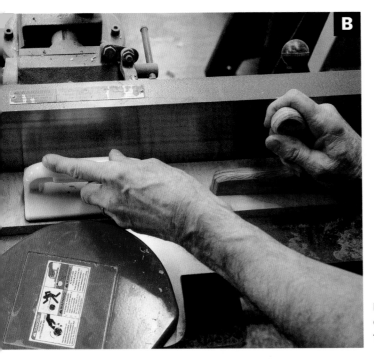

2. Smooth the bandsawn cut with the jointer. I set the depth of the jointer to take a shallow cut, and make a second cut if the first doesn't do the job. Sawing and then jointing the lids two at a time makes for safer handling in both operations. **(PHOTO B)**

FLATTEN THE BOX lid on the jointer to remove the bandsaw marks.

Prepare for the hinges

USING 5MM MINI BARREL HINGES TAKES some exacting work, as they must be perfectly aligned. To get the holes lined up exactly on both the lid and the base, I first make a story stick of thicker stock (in this case ¾-in. plywood) cut at the same time that I cut the lids to length using the crosscut sled and stop block. For this technique to work, the lid and story stick must be exactly the same length, so cutting them with the same setup is the best way to guarantee success. Since the base is shorter than the lid, drilling hinge holes in the base requires spacer blocks as a guide. I cut these from the same stock used to make the story stick. Cut the spacer blocks so that, when aligned at the ends of the box, they also align with the longer story stick. **(PHOTO A)** The more precise this step, the better, and you will find your touch more effective at discerning differences in length than your eyes alone.

STORY STICKS ARE important tools for locating the hinges. From front to back: angled lid, story stick (¾-in. ply), box with spacer blocks left and right.

If making more than two boxes, you may need to make more than one story stick, as slight variations in the length of boxes will cause misalignments in the setup and drilling of hinge holes.

Drill the hinge holes

1. Set up the drill press with a fence located so that the center of the drill is at the center of the ⅜-in. stock used for the box sides. A piece of scrap left over from making the sides can be useful for setting up this step. Mark the hinge location on the story stick and drill all the way through using a 5mm. brad-point bit. **(PHOTO A)**

2. With the drill still lowered into the hole, clamp a stop block on the left side of the fence while it is held against the story stick. Flip the story stick over with the same edge against the fence, and lower the drill into the hole. With the drill bit in the hole, clamp a stop block to the fence on the right, again with the stop block against the story stick. **(PHOTO B)**

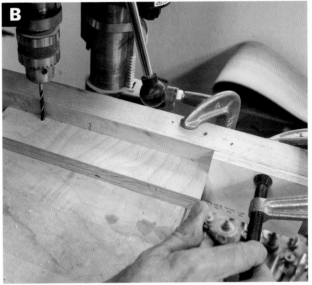

3. Drill the body of the box on the back edge with the box held against one spacer and stop block and then the other. Having the spacer in place on each side is essential to compensate for the longer lid. The depth of the hole should be carefully set to be no deeper than one-half the length of the hinge. **(PHOTO C)**

(TOP) DRILL ALL THE WAY through the story stick so it can be flipped and used in both directions.

(MIDDLE) FLIP THE STORY STICK with the same edge against the fence and align the drill bit into the hole to locate the position for the other stop block.

(BOTTOM) DRILL THE 5MM HOLES with the box against one stop block and then the other. Note that the spacer block is required in each position.

TO DRILL THE MATCHING HOLES in the lids, use one lid to prop up and level the other. The spacer blocks are not used as the lids are positioned against each stop block for drilling.

USE A CHAMFERING BIT in the router table to make the relief cut in the back edges of the lid and body of the box.

4. To drill matching holes in the lid, remove the spacers and double up the lids so that the lower one nested to the upper will hold it at a right angle. Again, the depth of the hole must be carefully set to drill no deeper than half the length of the hinge. **(PHOTO D)**

5. In order for the hinges to open, clearance must be provided in the form of a chamfer cut in both the top and bottom. The chamfer also provides a 90-degree stop when the lid is open, so it is both an attractive and useful feature. Use the router table and 45-degree chamfering bit to rout along the back edge of both the lid and body of the box. **(PHOTO E)**

Shape the lid

1. Make a simple template to mark the shape of the lid. Half a lid shape will do, and the template can be made from cardstock or thin plywood.

2. With the straight side of the template laid against the back edge of the box lid, trace and mark with pen or pencil, and then flip the template to create a symmetrical shape on the other end. **(PHOTO A)**

MAKE A PAPER OR WOOD TEMPLATE to help design the shape of the lid. Mark one end, flip the template, and then mark the other to achieve a symmetrical design.

3. Use the bandsaw to cut the lids to shape. **(PHOTO B)** Then sand the ends and front smooth and rout the edges.

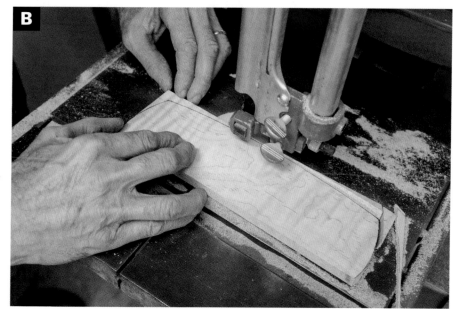

USE THE BANDSAW to cut the lids to shape.

Install the hinges

THE 5MM BARREL HINGES HAVE SMALL grooves along their length that allow them to be glued in place.

1. Use a squeeze bottle to apply just a bit of glue to the inside of the mounting holes before pushing the hinges in place. **(PHOTO A)**

APPLY A VERY SMALL AMOUNT of glue in the 5mm holes before inserting the hinges. Just a dab will lock the hinges in place.

2. Here you can see why careful alignment of holes in the lid and body of the box is essential. Gently nurse the hinges into the holes, being careful that they are going in at the right angle to be able to bend. Get both to seat fully in one part first, and then squeeze the lid and body of the box gradually to get them joined to each other. **(PHOTO B)**

CAREFULLY ALIGN THE HINGES and guide them into place as you squeeze the lid and the body of the box together.

More Ways to Add Rhythm

YOU MAY CHOOSE TO ADD RHYTHM TO A box in a variety of ways. Using different-colored woods as miter keys arranged in a specific pattern is one of the most obvious approaches, and this same technique of establishing a sense of rhythm and movement has been used on boxes throughout this book. The keys also convey a sense of craftsmanship. **(PHOTO A)**

Yet another interesting and often overlooked means of attaining rhythm is through the use of texture. The lid shown below, made from rough-sawn wood planed only on the inside and still with the patterns left by the original milling, can create a beautiful rhythmic effect. **(PHOTO B)** To make this lid, simply use a wire brush to finish the surface **(PHOTO C)** and remove loose

USE VISIBLE KEYS in the corners of a box to create a sense of rhythm.

ROUGH WOOD, left with marks of milling and weather, can create a sense of rhythm in a box.

material before applying the Danish oil finish. You can also employ rhythms of your own. For example, use an angle grinder to make random but rhythmic marks on plain-grained walnut to add additional character and interest. **(PHOTO D)** The use of dyes or ebonizing to turn the wood black can highlight the sense of rhythm you've created. For the box at bottom, I used a solution of vinegar with dissolved steel wool to ebonize (blacken) the walnut, which changed color due to a chemical reaction. **(PHOTO E)**

USE A WIRE BRUSH to remove loose material and fuzzy wood grain, while leaving the original saw marks and weathering.

WORK SMART

Put 1 Tbs. of 0000 steel wool in a pint of vinegar and allow it to sit overnight. Then use a sprayer or brush to apply the solution and watch as your wood turns black. Two applications may be required to get the darkest black color. Experiment with a sample of wood first, as ebonizing with vinegar and steel wool works only with some species, and individual samples of those species may react differently.

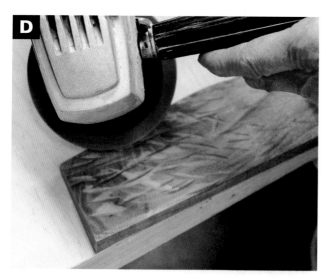

CREATE YOUR OWN TEXTURE to establish rhythm. An angle grinder with a 120-grit sanding disk can be applied in a rhythmic and varied texturing technique.

CREATE CONTRAST with stains and chemical treatments of wood. Apply ebonizing solution and watch walnut turn black.

A Finger-Jointed Chest

WITH THIS FINGER-
jointed chest, we'll
explore using propor-
tion in box design, which always
comes up when I teach boxmaking.
Boxmakers often wonder whether
there might be a set of proportions that would make the design
of boxes easier and the box itself
more beautiful. One formula of proportions that is always mentioned
by my students is based on the
Fibonacci series of numbers and
is variously called the golden ratio,
golden rectangle, or golden mean.
It is a ratio between length and
height or length and width of $\frac{1+\sqrt{5}}{2}$
commonly rounded as 1:1.62 or
1:1.618 . . . which was observed by
the ancient Greeks and centuries of
other art and architecture enthusi-
asts as having exceptional beauty.
In fact, the Greeks used the golden
rectangle to design the Parthenon,
and woodworkers and artists including Leonardo da Vinci have been
fascinated by the ratio as a curiosity
of design, finding examples of it
even in nature.

To see the exact shape in correct proportion, however, you must
stand in front and observe it dead
on, so a box that is viewed from
any number of angles may not be
the perfect candidate for its use. I
won't offer the formula as a sure-
fire way of making beautiful boxes.
I am willing, however, to present a
box based on the golden rectangle.

I'll let you decide if the golden rectangle imparts a special beauty to
this box. In any case, the box with
its angled dome lid draws on both
the look and proportion of classic
Greek architecture as its inspiration.
In this box, both the height and
depth (each 5½ in.) are in proportion to the length (excluding the
base) of 8⅞ in.

Finger-jointed chest

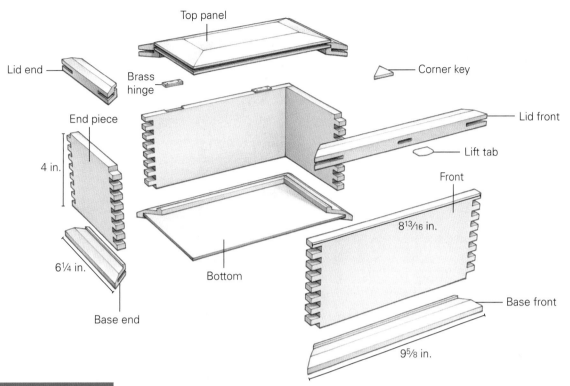

Top panel

Lid end

Brass hinge

Corner key

End piece

Lid front

4 in.

Lift tab

Front

$8^{13}/_{16}$ in.

$6^{1}/_{4}$ in.

Bottom

Base end

Base front

$9^{5}/_{8}$ in.

MATERIALS

QUANTITY	PART	MATERIAL	SIZE	NOTES
2	Front and back	Maple	$^{7}/_{16}$ in. x 4 in. x $8^{7}/_{8}$ in.*	
2	End pieces	Maple	$^{7}/_{16}$ in. x 4 in. x $5^{1}/_{2}$ in.*	
2	Base front and back	Maple	$^{1}/_{2}$ in. x 1 in. x $9^{5}/_{8}$ in.	
2	Base ends	Maple	$^{1}/_{2}$ in. x 1 in. x $6^{1}/_{4}$ in.	
1	Bottom	Baltic-birch plywood	$^{1}/_{8}$ in. x $4^{3}/_{4}$ in. x 8 in.	
2	Lid front and back	Maple	$^{5}/_{8}$ in. x 1 in. x $8^{13}/_{16}$ in.	
2	Lid ends	Maple	$^{5}/_{8}$ in. x 1 in. x $5^{7}/_{16}$ in.	
1	Top panel	Maple	$^{5}/_{8}$ in. x $4^{1}/_{4}$ in. x $7^{11}/_{16}$ in.	
4	Corner keys	Maple	$^{1}/_{8}$ in. x $1^{1}/_{4}$ in. x $1^{1}/_{4}$ in.	Triangles cut from $^{1}/_{8}$-in. x 1-in. maple stock
1 pair	Brass hinges	Narrow butt hinges	1 in. x $^{3}/_{4}$ in.	Ace Hardware number 5299730
1	Lift tab	Maple	$^{1}/_{8}$ in. x $^{1}/_{2}$ in. x $^{7}/_{8}$ in.	
1	Ball-chain lid support	3-in. number 3 ball chain and connectors		www.LeeValley.com stock number 00G48.01 for 6 sets

*length includes $^{1}/_{16}$-in. sanding allowance.

Proportion

PROPORTION IS ONE OF THE MORE FASCINATING
and controversial aspects of design. My students are
often interested in the golden ratio, a system of math-
ematical proportions discovered by the ancient Greeks
that promises a formula for achieving greater beauty.
Whether or not it actually does so may be in the eye
and position of the beholder. The Greek Parthenon is
an example of the deliberate use of the golden ratio,
but the magic proportion is visible only if you are standing exactly in front of the structure to see it head on.
View the Parthenon from one corner or the other, and,
regardless of the intentions of the ancient Greeks, what
you see will not be the golden ratio. The lead box in
this chapter is designed (looking down from the top)
according to the golden ratio. Its height and length are
also roughly to the same formula. But looking at the
box directly from one end or the other, there will be
no golden formula in sight. On a box it is impossible to
design each and every relationship between sides, top,
and bottom to fit the golden ratio, so a boxmaker looking for a simple means of proportion may need to look
beyond the ancient Greeks.

Besides the golden ratio there are other systems
of proportion in common use. For instance, one of my
favorites is a simple formula that can be expressed
as the ratio 1:1+/-2. In this simple plus-or-minus-two
formula one side equals the other plus or minus two.
From that simple formula you get common room sizes,
rug sizes, box sizes, and paper sizes that you will imme-
diately recognize: 3 by 5, 4 by 6, 5 by 7, 6 by 8, 7 by 9,
and 8 by 10, whether in inches or in feet. You will find
this system of proportion used on p. 39 and can judge
for yourself as to its merits.

On the other hand, you can try taking a more practical approach to your box design and attend to such
questions as what will fit inside, or where the box
might be used. For instance, you may have difficulty
finding a home on your desk for a large box, whereas a
smaller box may fit perfectly and hold your pens, pencils, and supplies. A deep box may not fit your hand as

**PROPORTION
CAN TAKE** its
cue from the object
the box is made to hold.
This elegant beaded bracelet and this box are a perfect
match.

easily as you reach inside,
whereas a shallow box may
present its contents in a
manner that makes small objects easier to find. And
so, for some, how the box will be used is the matter of
greatest concern with regard to proportion.

Besides size, there are other aspects of proportion that a boxmaker should consider in the design
of a box. Thick sides convey a sense of strength and
weight, while thin sides make for a more delicate box.
Then again, the type of hinge you have in mind may
dictate requirements of its own and demand that you
make your box with sides of sufficient thickness. For
instance, butt hinges work best and are easiest to
install accurately when they are mortised on three
sides, and they require thick enough material for
screws to lock tight.

A box consists of both inside and outside dimensions, and the proportions of each are important for
the boxmaker to consider. Thick sides reduce the useful volume of a box and add unnecessary weight. An
overly large interior space raises the question of how to
organize things inside. Dividing the inside of a box with
drawers or dividers may allow for the best use of the
inside proportions of the box and also allows the boxmaker to experiment with design.

Good proportion should be the goal of every box
you make, but I've found that there are no absolute
formulas or rules that will take the place of other considerations. Schemes of proportion can be most useful
if they help you to transition quickly through the design
process, put aside your creative hesitation, and get
busy making boxes in the woodshop.

One of the important things to consider about the proportions of a box is that it consists of both an outside shape and an inside space. So at the close of the chapter, I've offered two other boxes, both using the golden ratio as the starting point of design. One is equipped with sliding trays to make better use of the interior dimensions, and the other with a drawer, making the box more useful for keeping and storing small items.

I made this box with finger-jointed corners, a domed floating-panel lid, and a base that extends beyond the sides that is built with mitered parts that surround a piece of Baltic-birch plywood. An open space within that base allows for the addition of a secret compartment beneath a lined panel as shown in the box variation on p. 34.

Make a golden-ratio spacer block

MAKING AN APPROPRIATELY SIZED SPACER block for cutting the front, back, and ends of a golden-ratio box requires some simple math. Choose a length for the front and back and determine the length of the ends by multiplying that length by 0.62. Or you can choose the length of the ends and then determine the length of the front and back by multiplying that length by 1.618 (commonly rounded to 1.62). The length of the spacer block used for this box was determined by multiplying the length I'd chosen for the front and back of 8.875 by 0.62. The answer, 5.5025, rounds easily to 5½ for the short sides (and the height). My spacer block length was determined by subtracting 5½ in. from 8⅞ in. to get 3⅜ in. long.

Cut matching front, back, and ends from solid maple

AS IN THE LIFT-LID RECTANGULAR BOX, materials from thicker stock to make the best use of your available lumber. For this box, I resawed 1⅛-in. stock to obtain planed materials ⁷⁄₁₆ in. thick for the box sides. Slightly thinner sides would be acceptable.

1. To cut the box front, back, and ends in proportion to the golden rectangle in alternating cuts, you will need a spacer block 3⅜ in. long to use between cuts. First, cut the front of the box to the full length of 8⅞ in., with an extra ¹⁄₁₆ in. added in length to allow for just a bit of material to be sanded off the corners after assembly. **(PHOTO A)** Use the 90-degree crosscut sled and stop block to

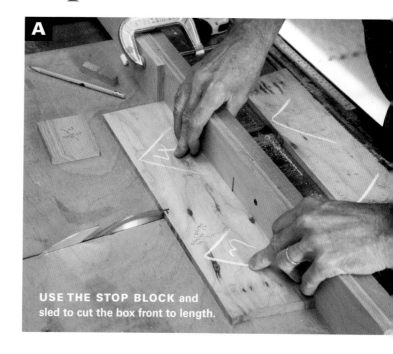

USE THE STOP BLOCK and sled to cut the box front to length.

B

USE A SPACER BLOCK to shorten the space
between the stop block and line of cut. For this box,
the spacer block is 3⅜ in. long, determined by using
the calculations on p. 93.

guarantee the perfect length. In the photo on p. 93
note the spacer block waiting for use in the next cut.

2. Make the next cut with the spacer block in
place between the stop block, the workpiece, and
the line of cut. **(PHOTO B)**

3. Remove the spacer block for the next
cut **(PHOTO C)** and put it back in place for
the final cut.

C

WITH THE SPACER BLOCK REMOVED, the box
back can be cut.

Form the finger joints to connect the sides

FINGER JOINTS ARE A VERY STRONG AND lasting way to make a box. The way the corners interlock makes a box nearly indestructible. I use a dedicated shopmade router table to cut finger joints (see p. 63), which allows me to leave things set up to make more boxes at the drop of a hat.

While I use a shopmade router table to rout the spaces between the fingers, this same operation can be done on the tablesaw using a sled and guide pin. Both can give excellent results, but the dedicated router setup leaves the tablesaw ready for other things. For the router-table method, use a ¼-in. spiral router bit raised to about 1/32 in. higher than the thickness of the stock. This allows for just a bit of length to be sanded from the fingers after the sides are glued and assembled.

1. Begin by placing the stock against the pin. Make repeat cuts, each time lifting the stock over the pin for the subsequent cut. You must be careful to start each end with the bottom edge of the stock against the pin. **(PHOTO A)**

2. After cutting the front and back, place a finger-jointed piece reversed on the jig so that one finger from the bottom edge overlaps the pin. This is necessary to index the first cut so that when the box is assembled, the parts will align at the top and bottom edges. With the indexing piece in place over the pin, you will form fingers on each end piece that will interlock with those already cut. Make a starting cut on each end piece, being careful again that the bottom edge is in place for the first cut. **(PHOTO B)**

USE A ROUTER TABLE SETUP for finger joints to cut the finger joints in the box front and back. The guide pin positions the stock for each cut.

FLIP ONE OF THE FIRST CUT PARTS over and use it to position the first matching cut in each of the box ends.

WITH THE INDEXING piece removed, make the subsequent cuts.

THE FINISHED FINGER JOINTS should fit together tightly without the use of a hammer to force them into place.

3. Once the first cuts have been made on each end piece, proceed to make the rest of the cuts just as you did on the front and back. **(PHOTO C)**

4. Your box should fit tightly together even before glue is applied, and it will last for as long as anyone finds it beautiful or useful enough to keep. **(PHOTO D)**

5. To glue the sides together, I use a squeeze bottle and apply a dab of glue to each finger. The applicator tip can be used to help spread the glue. **(PHOTO E)**

6. After gluing, check that the assembled box is square by measuring from one corner to another and comparing against the other diagonal. The corner-to-corner measurements should be the same. If not, squeeze the long corners together slightly to adjust. **(PHOTO F)**

7. After the glue has set, use a stationary belt sander or a sanding block to sand the fingers flush with the sides. **(PHOTO G)**

E

AFTER SANDING, use a squeeze bottle to apply glue to each finger as you prepare for assembly.

F

IF YOUR CORNERS FIT tightly, no clamps will be necessary, but be sure to measure from corner to corner in both directions. If both measurements are the same, the box will be square, just as you want it to be.

G

AFTER THE GLUE has dried, the edges can be sanded with a stationary belt sander or by laying a piece of coarse sandpaper flat on the benchtop.

Make the base

I USED THE MITER SLED TO MITER-FRAME
stock for the base and lid, and each is made in a
similar fashion. Use a stop block to control the
length of the parts.

1. Cut the mitered parts for the base. You can use
the same spacer block used in cutting the sides.
(PHOTO A) (Remember to change the stop block
setting when you cut the parts for the lid, as they
are intended to be the same length as the box sides
rather than the size of the base.)

2. Cut a groove into the edge of the front, back,
and ends of the base for a Baltic-birch plywood
panel to fit. A featherboard helps to hold the stock
tightly to the fence. Use a push stick to guide the
wood safely through the cut. **(PHOTO B)**

USE THE MITER SLED to begin making the base for
the box. The same spacer block used for making the box
sides can be used for this operation, or you can simply set
the stop block to the desired position for each cut.

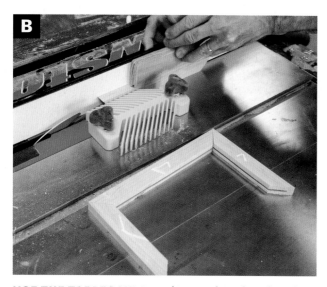

USE THE TABLESAW to make a cut into the edge of
each piece of the box base, ¾ in. deep to house the
bottom. A fingerboard and push stick make this
operation safe.

A picture-frame clamp works well to
hold the parts tight as the glue sets.
It is best to get the framing clamp
adjusted nearly to size before you
apply glue.

USE A STEEL RULE or tape measure
to determine the size for the Baltic-birch
plywood bottom.

SPREAD GLUE on the mitered corners and also apply a dab of glue inside the grooves at each corner.

3. Use a steel rule or tape measure to determine the exact size of the Baltic-birch plywood panel needed to fit the frame. I measure the inside of the cut to determine the length required. Cutting the Baltic-birch panel just a bit smaller in dimension than is actually required may make it easier to assemble with no loss of strength. **(PHOTO C)**

4. Prior to assembly, sand the Baltic-birch plywood panel and the inside edge of the bottom frame. You will have the opportunity to sand the rest later. I used a 45-degree chamfering bit on the router table to chamfer the inside edges on both the top and bottom of each piece.

5. Use a squeeze bottle to apply glue to the mitered surfaces. Also apply a bit of glue to the inside of the grooves at the ends so that the Baltic-birch plywood panel will add strength to the base construction. **(PHOTO D)**

USE A CORNER CLAMP to pull the corners tight as the glue sets. Observe closely to make certain the edges are also flat.

6. Use a picture-frame clamp to pull the parts of the bottom tight until after the glue sets. Clamps that pull equally from all corners like the one shown above are great for boxmaking. **(PHOTO E)**

7. Cut a shelf for the assembled box sides to fit the base. This small cut gives a place for the sides to exactly fit the base, making it easier and more precise when it comes time to glue the base in place. An accessory fence keeps the blade from cutting into the standard fence. Raise the blade height through a series of cuts until the assembled box nests neatly in place in the base. **(PHOTO F)**

8. To trim the base angles, move the fence and tilt the blade to 15 degrees. This step will lighten the appearance of the box base and give it a more finished look. **(PHOTO G)**

USE THE TABLESAW and accessory fence to make a cut along each side of the box base assembly so that the box sides will nest neatly on it.

THEN TILT THE BLADE to 15 degrees to trim the base assembly to shape, but be careful to leave the flat area uncut to nest the box sides.

Make the domed or angled lid

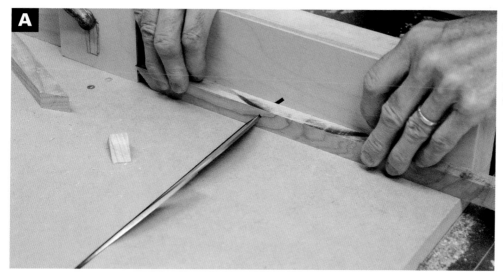

CUT THE PARTS for the box lid in the same manner used to make the base.

AN ANGLED DOME LID GIVES THIS BOX A classic look in keeping with its Greek proportions. The shape of the lid is architecturally inspired and intended to establish a visual connection between the box and the use of the golden mean in Greek architecture.

1. Cut the lid front, back, and sides to the same lengths as the front, back, and ends of the box. The same spacer block used in cutting the front, back, and ends of the box can be used to alternate between cuts. **(PHOTO A)**

2. Tape the parts together and measure the opening to determine the size of the top panel. **(PHOTO B)** Add ⅜ in. to the length to allow for a ³⁄₁₆-in. tongue at each end. Add ¹⁄₃₂ in. less than ⅜ in. to the measured width. This will allow room for any expansion that might occur in very humid conditions.

3. The floating panel lid for this box fits into grooves cut in the inside edges of the lid frame. For this method to work, the tongue and groove on the edge of the top panel must exactly match

the tongue and groove on the inside edges of the lid frame, and the tongue and groove must be the same size, in this case, ⅛ in. After you cut the top panel to size (see the materials list for thickness, but rely on your measurements for length and width), adjust the saw so that the height of cut is ³⁄₁₆ in. and the distance from the fence to the blade is ⅛ in. I use a blade designed to give a square-topped cut to make things easier to measure and to get a better fit. Make a series of test cuts if necessary.

TRIAL ASSEMBLE THE BOX LID FRAME and close the corners tightly with tape so that you can accurately measure the size of the floating panel for the top.

4. When two pieces of scrap wood will slide together easily as shown, the relationship between the top panel and sides can be cut for a perfect fit. **(PHOTO C)**

5. Use push sticks or a push block and featherboard to guide the lid sides through the cut. Note that the undersides of the lid sides are held against the fence. **(PHOTO D)**

6. Cutting the matching grooves in the floating panel requires that it also be held tightly against the fence. The same notched push stick held flat

AFTER CUTTING THE TOP PANEL to size, set up the tablesaw to make the cuts to join the top panel to the frame parts. Two parts cut in the setup should nest together.

USE PUSH STICKS to guide the lid frame parts across the tablesaw to make the grooves to fit the top panel.

on the surface of the saw will hold the panel tightly to the fence and guide it through the cut. Cut the end grain first and then the side grain so that the side grain cut will remove any tearout that could cause difficulties at the time of assembly. **(PHOTO E)**

7. To make the angled cuts that form the domed lid, I use a shopmade tenon-cutting jig that slides along the tablesaw fence. Tilt the blade to 15 degrees and set the distance from the fence so that about ⅛ in. or slightly less of the edge remains. **(PHOTO F)** Cut the ends first and then the sides. For best results and to avoid error, push the lid past the blade and then shut down the saw and wait for it to stop before removing your finished workpiece.

8. Sand the inside surface of the top panel and the inside edges of the frame before assembly. I routed the inside edges of the frame with a 45-degree chamfering bit to give it a more finished look.

9. To glue the lid assembly, use a squeeze bottle to apply glue to the mitered surfaces of each part, and put just a dab of glue in the groove at the centers of the end pieces. **(PHOTO G)** This

USE A PUSH STICK to guide the top panel through the cut. Cut the ends first and then the sides.

is to hold the panel at the center of the assembly so that it doesn't slide around from one side or the other during very dry weather. Only a small spot of glue is needed to keep the panel centered. More might interfere with the normal expansion and contraction of wood.

USE A SHOPMADE TENONING JIG to guide the top panel as you cut the angle in the top. Cut the ends first and then the sides.

APPLY GLUE to the miters and just a dab at the center of each end piece to hold the floating panel centered in the lid frame.

USE A FRAME CLAMP to hold the lid parts tightly as the glue sets.

10. Use a frame clamp to hold the parts tightly together as the glue dries. You can also use tape and rubber bands for this operation as shown on p. 29. **(PHOTO H)**

11. After the glue dries, use the tablesaw with the angle set at 20 degrees to trim the edges of the lid to shape. The amount of wood remaining on the front edge should be ½ in. Set the blade height carefully to avoid touching the floating panel. An accessory high fence can make this a more comfortable operation. **(PHOTO I)**

12. I use keys in the corners of the lid of this box just as I did in the veneered boxes. Use a simple jig as shown to guide the lid through the cut held at a 45-degree angle in relation to the saw. **(PHOTO J)**

13. Glue matching maple keys in place. **(PHOTO K)**

14. Sand the keys flush with the edges of the lid. This can be done with either a stationary belt sander or with a coarse sanding block. **(PHOTO L)**

TRIM THE EDGES of the lid to shape with the saw blade tilted to 20 degrees.

USE A KEYED MITER JIG on the tablesaw to cut grooves in the corners of the lid for miter keys to fit.

GLUE THE CORNER keys in place on the lid.

K

L

Finishing Touches

TO FINISH THE BOX, INSTALL HINGES AND A simple lift tab using the story-stick method demonstrated on p. 53. I used a ball chain to control the opening of the lid so that it doesn't fall back too far. To attach the base, lay a bead of glue along the inside edge of the lip and clamp it in place. If you want to make a secret compartment in the bottom, apply lining material to a piece of ⅛-in. Baltic-birch plywood cut to a size only slightly smaller than the interior dimension of the box. A small tab of matching lining material extending from one end allows for it to be removed, revealing the hidden space below. Apply Danish oil to bring out the beauty of the wood and to protect that beauty for years to come.

SAND THE EDGES of the lid until the keys are flush. This operation can also be done easily with a coarse sanding block.

Add a Drawer

IN MAKING A BOX, THE EXTERIOR PROPOR-
tions are not the boxmaker's only concern. What will fit
inside and how that will be arranged are also important
considerations. A small box will naturally hold small
things. A large box can be designed to hold something
large or a mess of smaller things. In order to make a
box more useful, the interior proportions can be engi-
neered by adding trays, dividers, drawers, and other
components.

The variations in this chapter are intended to illustrate
opportunities to make better use of the interior space
within a box. In the first example, a box made of pin oak,
in the same proportions as the maple box, is made with
a drawer. This design also gives a shallow interior depth
from which small items can be easily retrieved. Another
option is to add sliding trays to the interior of the box
(see p. 114). Depending on whether you want the trays to
slide from front to back or side to side, strips of wood are
affixed to provide support.

Finger-jointed box with drawer

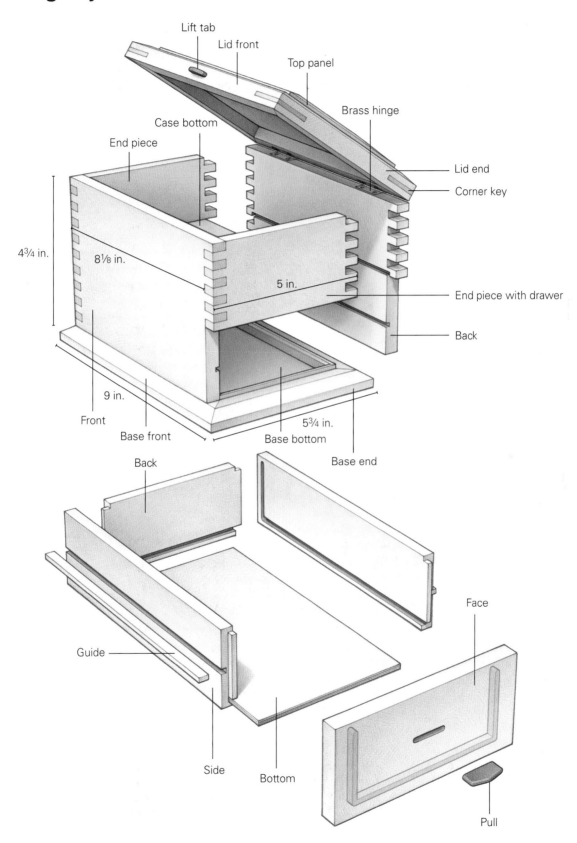

Lift tab

Lid front

Top panel

Brass hinge

Case bottom

End piece

Lid end

Corner key

$4^{3}/_{4}$ in.

$8^{1}/_{8}$ in.

5 in.

End piece with drawer

Back

9 in.

Front

Base front

$5^{3}/_{4}$ in.

Base bottom

Base end

Back

Guide

Side

Bottom

Face

Pull

MATERIALS

QUANTITY	PART	MATERIAL	SIZE	NOTES
2	Front and back	White oak	$7/16$ in. x $4\frac{3}{4}$ in. x $8\frac{3}{16}$ in.*	
1	End piece with drawer	White oak	$7/16$ in. x $2\frac{3}{8}$ in. x $5\frac{1}{16}$ in.*	
1	End piece	White oak	$7/16$ in. x $4\frac{3}{4}$ in. x $5\frac{1}{16}$ in.*	
1	Case bottom	Baltic-birch plywood	$\frac{1}{8}$ in. x $4\frac{3}{8}$ in. x $7\frac{1}{2}$ in.	
2	Base front and back	White oak	$\frac{1}{2}$ in. x 1 in. x 9 in.	
2	Base ends	White oak	$\frac{1}{2}$ in. x 1 in. x $5\frac{3}{4}$ in.	
1	Base bottom	Baltic-birch plywood	$\frac{1}{8}$ in. x $5\frac{1}{4}$ in. x $8\frac{5}{8}$ in.	
2	Lid front and back	White oak	$\frac{5}{8}$ in. x 1 in. x $8\frac{1}{8}$ in.	
2	Lid ends	White oak	$\frac{5}{8}$ in x 1 in. x 5 in.	
1	Top panel	White oak	$\frac{5}{8}$ in. x $3\frac{7}{8}$ in. x 7 in.	
4	Corner keys	White oak	$\frac{1}{8}$ in. x $1\frac{1}{4}$ in. x $1\frac{1}{4}$ in.	Triangles cut from $\frac{1}{8}$-in. x 1-in. stock
1 pair	Brass hinges	Narrow butt hinges	1 in. x $\frac{3}{4}$ in.	Ace Hardware number 5299730
1	Lift tab	Walnut	$\frac{1}{8}$ in. x $\frac{1}{2}$ in. x $\frac{3}{4}$ in.	
1	Ball-chain lid support	3-in. number 3 ball chain and connectors		

DRAWER PARTS

QUANTITY	PART	MATERIAL	SIZE	NOTES
1	Face	White oak	$7/16$ in. x $2\frac{3}{8}$ in. x $5\frac{1}{16}$ in.*	
2	Slides	Maple	$\frac{5}{16}$ in x 2 in. x $7\frac{9}{16}$ in	
1	Back	Maple	$\frac{5}{16}$ in. x 2 in. x $3\frac{7}{8}$ in.	
1	Bottom	Baltic-birch plywood	$\frac{1}{8}$ in. x $3\frac{3}{4}$ in. x $7\frac{1}{4}$ in.	
2	Guides	Maple	$\frac{1}{8}$ in. x $\frac{1}{4}$ in. x $7\frac{3}{8}$ in.	

*length includes $1/16$-in. sanding allowance.

TO MAKE A BOX with a drawer, first mark the location of the fingers on the box parts. I use pencil or chalk so that any residue will sand away.

CUT ONLY AS many fingers as necessary and stop. Then cut matching parts.

MAKE A BOX WITH A DRAWER

1. Begin by carefully laying out the fingers required. Note that not as many are necessary on the end where the drawer fits. Mark carefully. **(PHOTO A)**

2. Cut the finger joints only partway up as shown on the end where the drawer will pull open. A trial assembly helps to check the fit before you move on to the next step. **(PHOTO B)**

3. Use a ⅛-in. router bit in the router table to rout grooves in the front, back, and ends for the case bottom to fit, and then in the front and back for the drawer guides. You will need to set up the height of the router bit at ⅛ in. and plan your routing on the long sides so that the groove passes safely between fingers. **(PHOTO C)**

TO ROUT FOR THE CASE bottom and drawer guides, use a ⅛-in. router bit and set up the fence so that the router bit can pass between the fingers without touching.

FOR THE CASE BOTTOM to fit, the ends as well as the front and back must be routed. Set the fence so that the cut will be made the correct distance from the top edge, and use stop blocks so that as you rout, the bit will not cut through the fingers.

4. The grooves on the ends that house the bottom of the upper compartment must be routed between stops as shown below. **(PHOTO D)**

5. After the bottom panel has been cut to size, the box will be ready for sanding inside and assembly. **(PHOTO E)**

AS YOU CAN SEE in the trial-assembled box, only the long sides of the box need to be routed for the drawer guide strips. Position the grooves between fingers.

Make the drawer

I USED SIMPLE MORTISE-AND-TENON joinery for the drawer in this box, employing a router table technique in which the mortise is formed with a ⅛-in. straight-cut router bit, routing between stops. Cut one mortise on each drawer side, and the remaining ones in the drawer face to connect it with the sides of the drawer.

Rout the mortises

MAKING A DRAWER TO FIT IN A BOX CAN take careful calculation and measurement. In order for the drawer front to overlay the sides of the box, the mortises for the drawer sides and for the drawer front must be routed with the router table fence in two different positions.

1. Rout the drawer sides between stops, with the height of the router bit raised to ³⁄₁₆ in. and the fence set so that the outside point of the router cut is slightly greater than the thickness of the stock being used to make the drawer parts. **(PHOTO F)**

TO FORM THE DRAWER MORTISES, use a ⅛-in. straight-cut router bit with fence and stop blocks to guide the workpiece.

MOVE THE FENCE to rout the mortises in the drawer front. The stop blocks will also need to be adjusted for this operation.

2. Change the location of the fence to rout the mortises in the drawer front. In order to do this accurately, you will also need to change the position of the stop blocks. **(PHOTO G)**

Form the tenons

THE NEXT STEP IN MAKING DRAWER PARTS, forming tenons on the router table, can be tricky. Stand the stock on end and pass it along the router table between the router bit and fence. The safety blocking, which consists of one block of wood standing away from the cutter covered by another that completely covers the cutter (absolutely required), obscures the operation as the stock is moved from right to left. **(PHOTO H)** The photo at right shows the setup with blocking removed for a better view. **(PHOTO I)**

TO CUT THE TENONS on the drawer sides and back, use the router table and a large straight-cut bit. (Note that the operation here, as parts are moved along the fence right to left, is hidden by necessary safety blocking that covers the router bit.)

WORK
SMART

A "climb-feed" cut, in which the wood can be grabbed by the rotation of the cutter and pulled into the cut, should be used only when making a shallow cut and only when safety blocking is in place.

FORMING THE TENONS accurately requires passing the stock between the router bit and fence, something not to be tried when taking a larger cut. In this photo, the safety blocking has been removed.

ROUT THE GROOVES for the bottom panel using a ⅛-in. router bit, raised ⅛ in. above the router table top. Use stop blocks to keep the routed groove from appearing on the out-side of the drawer.

1. Form the tenons on each end of the drawer back and on the unmortised end of the drawer sides. Then use the ⅛-in. router bit to rout for the drawer bottom to fit. For the drawer sides and drawer front, stop blocks will be required to make blind cuts that don't appear on the outside of the drawer. **(PHOTO J)**

2. To make the tenoned ends of the drawer parts fit the mortises in the sides and drawer front, the tenon width must be narrowed using the sled and stop block on the tablesaw. Adjust the stop block to nibble away on both the top and bottom edges enough for the tenons to fit cleanly into the mortises. For the cleanest cuts and to avoid trapping material between the blade and the stop block, make the first cuts with the workpiece slightly

USE THE TABLESAW crosscut sled and a stop block to nibble away the tenons to the correct width to fit the mortises in the sides and drawer front.

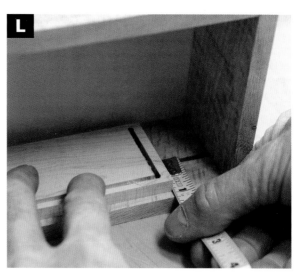

MEASURE CAREFULLY to determine the location for the drawer-guide grooves to fit the drawer sides.

TO DETERMINE THE LOCATION of the groove to house the drawer bottom in the drawer front, put the drawer parts in place (including the drawer guides), and measure the distance from the edge of the drawer end to the edge of the Baltic-birch plywood.

ROUT THE DRAWER front to allow the ⅛-in. Baltic-birch plywood bottom to fit.

THE DRAWER is an interesting and attractive feature and also makes the box more useful. Add a pull of your own selection or design

away from the stop block and then the second cut on each side with the workpiece pushed firmly in place. **(PHOTO K)**

Cut the drawer-guide grooves

1. Determining the location of the drawer-guide grooves in the sides of the drawer requires careful measuring. Line up the drawer inside the box, and then measure from the groove cut to house the drawer guide in the side of the box to the bottom edge of the drawer as you hold it in the desired position. Use this measurement to set up the router table fence to rout the drawer-guide grooves in the drawer sides. **(PHOTO L)**

2. After the drawer-guide grooves are routed in the sides, measure to find the position of the groove in the drawer front for the drawer bottom to fit. **(PHOTO M)**

3. Use the measurement from step 2 to set up the router table to cut the groove for the bottom. **(PHOTO N)**

4. Check the fit of the drawer before gluing the corners and gluing the drawer guides in place. **(PHOTO O)**

Include a Sliding Tray

MAKING A SIMPLE SLID-
ing tray is similar to making
a small box like the Lift-Lid
Rectangular Box. But in order
to install a tray, you have to
think ahead and allow for the
tray to fit before the box is
assembled. Cut grooves for
tray supports in either the ends
or the front and back of the
box as was shown in making
drawer-guide grooves on p.
109. This groove is most easily cut between fingers on a
finger-jointed box and can be
done either on the tablesaw or
the router table to a depth of
about ⅛ in.

MATERIALS

QUANTITY	PART	MATERIAL	SIZE	NOTES
2	Front and back	Cherry	$\frac{7}{16}$ in. x $3\frac{1}{4}$ in. x $9\frac{3}{4}$ in.*	
2	End pieces	Cherry	$\frac{7}{16}$ in. x $3\frac{1}{4}$ in. x $6\frac{1}{16}$ in. thick*	
2	Base front and back	Cherry	$\frac{5}{8}$ in. x 1 in. x $10\frac{1}{2}$ in.	
2	Base ends	Cherry	$\frac{5}{8}$ in. x 1 in. x $6\frac{13}{16}$ in.	
1	Bottom	Baltic-birch plywood	$\frac{1}{8}$ in. x $6\frac{1}{4}$ in. x 10 in.	
2	Lid front and back	Cherry	$\frac{5}{8}$ in. x 1 in. x $9\frac{11}{16}$ in.	
2	Lid ends	Cherry	$\frac{5}{8}$ in. x 1 in. x 6 in.	
1	Lip panel	Cherry	$\frac{5}{8}$ in. x $4\frac{7}{8}$ in. x $8\frac{5}{8}$ in.	

*length includes $\frac{1}{16}$-in. sanding allowance.

Box with a sliding tray

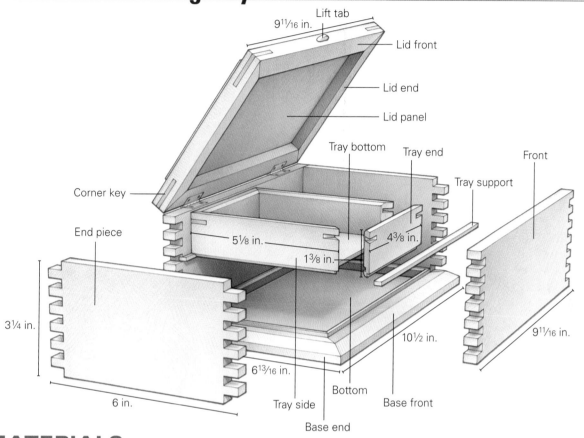

Lift tab

9^{11}/$_{16}$ in.

Lid front

Lid end

Lid panel

Tray bottom

Tray end

Tray support

Front

Corner key

End piece

5^{1}/$_{8}$ in.

4^{3}/$_{8}$ in.

1^{3}/$_{8}$ in.

3^{1}/$_{4}$ in.

6^{13}/$_{16}$ in.

Tray side

Bottom

Base end

Base front

10^{1}/$_{2}$ in.

9^{11}/$_{16}$ in.

6 in.

MATERIALS (CONTINUED)

QTY	PART	MATERIAL	SIZE	NOTES
4	Corner keys	Cherry	^{1}/$_{8}$ in. x 1^{1}/$_{4}$ in. x 1^{1}/$_{4}$ in.	Triangles cut from ^{1}/$_{8}$-in. x 1-in. stock
1	Lift tab	Cherry	^{1}/$_{8}$ in. x ^{1}/$_{2}$ in. x ^{3}/$_{4}$ in.	
1 pair	Brass hinges	Narrow butt hinges	1 in. x ^{3}/$_{4}$ in.	Ace Hardware number 5299730
1	Ball-chain lid support			www.LeeValley.com stock number 00G48.01 for 6 sets
2	Tray sides	Cherry	^{5}/$_{16}$ in. x 1^{3}/$_{8}$ in. x 5^{1}/$_{8}$ in.	
2	Tray ends	Cherry	^{5}/$_{16}$ in. x 1^{3}/$_{8}$ in. x 4^{3}/$_{8}$ in.	
1	Tray bottom	Baltic-birch plywood	^{1}/$_{8}$ in. x 4 in. x 4^{3}/$_{4}$ in.	
4	Corner keys	Cherry	^{5}/$_{8}$ in. x ^{5}/$_{8}$ in.	Triangles cut from ^{1}/$_{8}$-in. x ^{1}/$_{2}$-in. stock
2	Tray supports	Cherry	^{1}/$_{8}$ in. x ^{5}/$_{16}$ in. x 8^{13}/$_{16}$ in.	

A

TO MAKE A sliding tray for a box, use the 45-degree miter sled and stop blocks to cut the sides to length.

Make the tray

1. Cut the tray parts to length and miter the corners of each piece. (You will note that for this tray I cut the groove to house the bottom panel before cutting the parts.) Tilt the saw to 45 degrees and use the miter sled and stop block to control the length of matching parts. **(PHOTO A)**

2. Glue and assemble the sides around the bottom panel and, after the glue has set, cut miter key slots in the corners to give additional strength. **(PHOTO B)**

3. Glue the miter keys in place. These can be either matching wood, as I am using here, or wood of a contrasting color for more decorative effect. **(PHOTO C)**

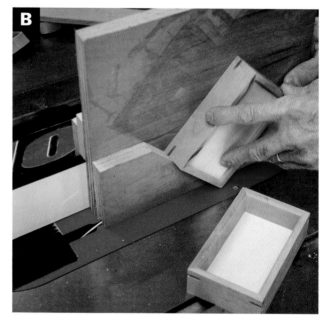

B

AFTER CUTTING THE TRAY BOTTOM to fit and gluing the corners together, cut miter key slots on the tablesaw. (You can make a second tray following the same directions.)

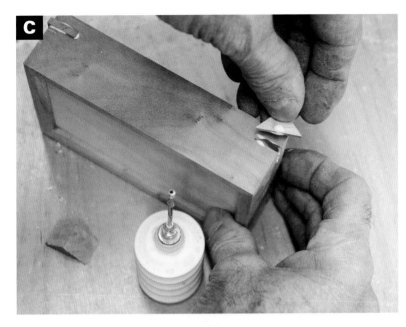

4. Finally, cut the bottom edges of the tray to fit neatly over the runners. **(PHOTO D)**

APPLY GLUE and insert the keys.

MAKE A SMALL ROUTED STRAIGHT CUT along the bottom edge so that the tray will fit over the guide strips. (If you make a second tray, fit it the same way.)

A Jewelry Box

MAKING A JEWELRY box with a drawer and dividers is more complicated than most boxes and requires a higher level of attention and skill. This box, with mitered corners that have been secured with dowels, illustrates how to use and accentuate texture. The dowels used to secure the corners draw the eye and invite the fingers to touch. The random pattern carved in the top not only causes the light to dance on the surface of the box but also invites the fingers to explore. In the design variations of this box, I've used multiple layers of milk paint to highlight surface effects carved into the wood. On another variation, a simple relief carving adds a textural dimension to the design. Of course, not everyone will like the dowels used to secure the joints. Instead, you can use any of the joinery techniques in this book, or with practice you can make this same box using mitered hand-cut dovetails.

One little surprise in this box is that the drawer covers a secret compartment for letters or love notes.

Jewelry box

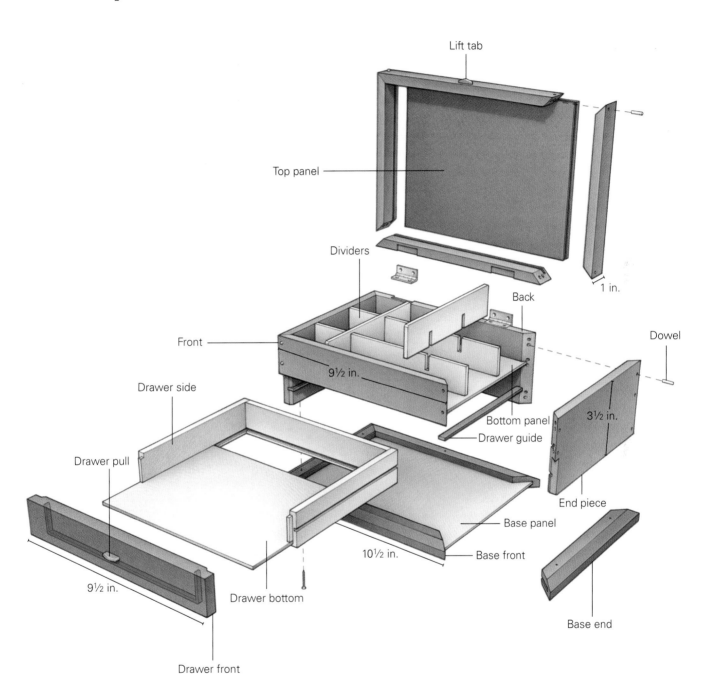

Lift tab

Top panel

Dividers

Back

Front

9½ in.

1 in.

Dowel

Drawer side

Bottom panel

Drawer guide

3½ in.

Drawer pull

Base panel

End piece

9½ in.

10½ in.

Base front

Drawer bottom

Base end

Drawer front

MATERIALS

QUANTITY	PART	MATERIAL	SIZE	NOTES
1	Front	Walnut	$7/16$ in. x 3 in. x $9\frac{1}{2}$ in.	Cut to finished height after mitering.
1	Back	Walnut	$7/16$ in. x $4\frac{5}{8}$ in. x $9\frac{1}{2}$ in.	
2	End pieces	Walnut	$7/16$ in. x $4\frac{5}{8}$ in. x $7\frac{1}{2}$ in.	
1	Top panel	Painted basswood	$\frac{1}{2}$ in. x $6^{15}/16$ in. x 9 in.	
1	Bottom panel	Baltic-birch plywood	$\frac{1}{8}$ in. x 7 in. x 9 in.	
36	Dowels	Hardwood	$\frac{1}{8}$ in. x $\frac{5}{8}$ in. approx.	Cut to depth of holes plus $\frac{1}{8}$ in.
2	Base front and back	Basswood	$\frac{5}{8}$ in. x 1 in. x $10\frac{1}{2}$ in.	
2	Base ends	Basswood	$\frac{5}{8}$ in. x 1 in. x $8\frac{1}{2}$ in.	
1	Base panel	Baltic-birch plywood	$\frac{1}{8}$ in. x $7\frac{3}{4}$ in. x $9\frac{3}{4}$ in.	
2	Drawer sides	Hard maple or other hardwood	$5/16$ in. x $1\frac{1}{2}$ in. x $6^{13}/16$ in.	
1	Drawer back	Hard maple or other hardwood	$5/16$ in. x $1\frac{1}{2}$ in. x $8\frac{3}{8}$ in.	
1	Drawer front	Basswood	$9/16$ in. x $1^9/16$ in. x $9\frac{1}{2}$ in.	
1	Drawer bottom	Baltic-birch plywood	$\frac{1}{8}$ in. x $6\frac{1}{2}$ in. x $8\frac{1}{4}$ in.	
2	Drawer guides	Hard maple or other hardwood	$\frac{1}{8}$ in. x $\frac{3}{8}$ in. x $6\frac{3}{4}$ in.	Cut at angle in front to fit drawer.
1 pair	Hinges	Brusso solid brass butt hinges	$1\frac{1}{4}$ in.	Woodcraft®, Rockler®, or Lee Valley
5	Screws	Black sheet rock screws	#6 1 in. long	
1	Stock for pulls and lift tabs	Walnut	$\frac{1}{8}$-in. x $\frac{1}{2}$-in. x 3-in. stock	Shape to fit as you please.
2	Left to right dividers	Basswood or other light hardwood	$3/16$ in. x $8\frac{5}{8}$ in. x $1\frac{3}{8}$ in.	
2	Front to back dividers	Basswood or other light hardwood	$3/16$ in. x $6^9/16$ in. x $1\frac{1}{2}$ in.	

Texture

TEXTURE IS ONE OF THE essential design tools that can be used to make beautiful boxes. Just as the use of various colors of wood can add interest to a box, so too can the use of various textures. The hand and eye are both involved in the exploration of surface texture. When the eyes see something that attracts them, the hands instinctively reach out to touch that object. Touch is a process of exploration, and texture is the invitation.

To plane or sand a surface smooth is one of the greatest pleasures to be found in woodworking. It offers immediate feedback to the craftsman and gives a sense of personal satisfaction as the work at hand moves from coarse to smooth. And again, when the viewer of a finely crafted box sees an engaging surface, like the satiny smooth surface of a well-sanded box, his or her hands will be called into action.

Wood grain often offers the illusion of texture. Through the reflection and refraction of light, woods like curly maple may appear to be made up of varying depths. Careful sanding and finish can accentuate those depths, surprising viewers when they run their hands over the surface only to discover it is perfectly smooth to the touch. That kind of surprise is particularly effective in the design of a beautiful box.

Smooth and rough textures are equally useful in the making of beautiful boxes. Many woodworkers have become so intent on achieving smooth surfaces that they overlook the alternatives. Rough textures present many interesting design options. Woods, as they come direct from the sawmill, often present textures that can be used to make boxes that are beautiful, and surprising. Woods that are old and weathered

TEXTURE, WHETHER FORMED BY NATURE or by tools, can capture the eye and engage the touch. The rhythmic texture on the lid of this box is formed by the huge saw blade cutting lumber from the log.

tell a story of their own and can also add interest to a box. When using rough woods, however, sand them just enough to be smooth to the touch.

Textures you make yourself through the use of various tools like grinders, rasps, and gouges will make a plain piece of wood more visually appealing, and creating these textures can be part of the fun of boxmaking. Again, sand your work smooth to the touch but not enough to remove your carefully crafted marks.

I find it particularly exciting to juxtapose purposefully rough or textured surfaces with those that are perfectly smooth as a way of creating contrast in a box, just as I might choose to use two distinct colors of wood. When making a box that you hope will attract both hand and eye, the use of texture is a design tool that should not be overlooked. It will help you to create beautiful boxes.

Prepare the stock

TO BE THRIFTY IN THE USE OF MATERIALS, I resawed the wood for the sides of this box from full 1-in.-thick walnut, and the material for the top panel, drawer front, and base frame was planed to dimension from basswood. I used hard maple (resawn from thicker stock) for the drawer sides and drawer guides for long life and precise operation. I used ⅛-in. Baltic-birch plywood for the bottom panel and drawer bottom for lighter weight and stability.

Miter the corners

1. After resawing stock for the sides, joint one edge on the jointer and then cut the parts to width. Miter the corners and cut the box sides to length using the miter sled on the tablesaw as shown on p. 24. Check with the materials list on p. 120 for the exact sizes of these parts. I used a 2-in. spacer block to set the proportion between the length of the sides and ends to correspond to the ratio x:x +/- 2 as done in the veneered box.

2. Once the box sides are mitered, check to see that they fit together tightly, and apply tape to the corners so that the top panel can be measured and cut to size. Measure the inside space in both directions and add ⅜ in. to each for the length of the top panel and the tongues that will extend into the grooves on the inside edges of the box sides.

Fit the top panel to the sides

1. Use the tablesaw to cut a groove in the sides to fit the top panel. Raise the height of the blade to ³⁄₁₆ in. The space between the blade and the fence must equal the width of the sawkerf; I make trial-and-error practice cuts on scrap wood to make sure that the top panel and sides fit neatly and smoothly together. Measure carefully to make certain that the cut is deep enough. You will not want to force the fit. **(PHOTO A)**

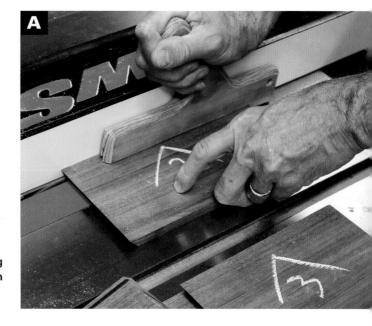

SET THE HEIGHT of the tablesaw blade to ³⁄₁₆ in. and set the space between the blade and the fence to ⅛ in. Then cut along the inside face of each mitered side to form the groove for the floating top panel.

MAKE THE SAME CUT along the edge of the top panel with the inside face against the fence.

2. Hold the top panel along the fence to cut the groove in the edges to fit the grooves cut in the sides. In this simple technique, matching tongue and grooves are formed in the same operation—the tongue by the space between the fence and blade, and the groove by the blade itself. I cut the groove in the ends first and then the sides so that the last cuts will remove any splintered wood. **(PHOTO B)**

3. With the blade still set at ³⁄₁₆ in. high, make additional cuts in the box ends and front and back for the bottom to fit.

Prepare for the drawer to fit

1. With the tablesaw blade still set at the height of ³⁄₁₆ in., cut the grooves for the drawer guides. **(PHOTO A)** This cut should be made only in the two ends (it's unnecessary in the front or back).

MAKE ADDITIONAL CUTS in the box ends for the ¹⁄₈-in.-thick drawer guides to fit.

2. After the grooves are cut, the front of the box can be cut to its finished height, which allows space for the drawer to fit in the front of the box. **(PHOTO B)**

3. Note in the drawing and photo of the finished box that I've squared off the front edge of the box sides where the drawers come to rest in a closed position. Cut away 5/16 in. at the front edge of the left and right sides of the box, with the blade raised to the height of the drawer front. This allows for a more secure fit for the drawer front and prevents a vulnerable miter edge being exposed to wear or damage. **(PHOTO C)**

4. Sand the insides of the box including the ends, front, and back so they will be ready for assembly. **(PHOTO D)**

CUT THE FRONT PIECE to its smaller size to allow for the drawer.

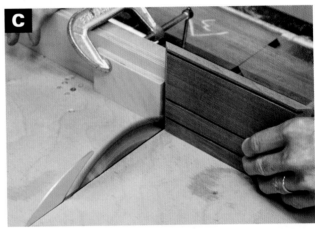

CUT THE FRONT edge of the box sides to allow for the drawer front. The blade height needs to be set carefully to cut no higher than the opening for the drawer.

SAND THE INSIDE surfaces of the box front, ends, and back.

Texture the top panel

ADDING TEXTURE TO WOOD IS A GREAT way to add interest to your box. I used an angle grinder with a medium-grit sanding disc to make random markings on the basswood top panel.

1. Make sure the wood is firmly clamped in place, allowing you to keep both hands on the tool and safe from injury. I make a light, seemingly random, tapping motion with the tool. **(PHOTO A)**

2. To prepare for painting, sand all the surfaces of the top panel smooth, being careful to preserve the texture you've just created. Paint will call attention to irregularities in surface qualities, so the inside will need to be carefully sanded. And even though the outside is textured, it still needs to be lightly sanded, most particularly on the exposed edges.

3. Use spray paint to turn the top panel black **(PHOTO B)** (or you can try milk paints as shown in the variations at the close of this chapter).

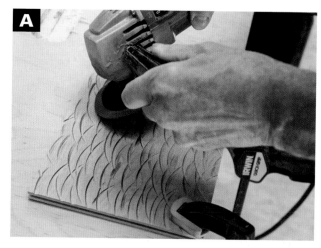

USE AN ANGLE GRINDER with a sanding disk to texture the top panel. Clamp the top panel firmly to the workbench and keep both hands on the grinder for safety and maximum control.

USE BLACK ENAMEL SPRAY PAINT to color the top panel.

Assemble the box

SPREAD GLUE ON THE MITERED SUR- faces and assemble the box sides around the bottom and lid panel. **(PHOTO A)** Use tape, rubber bands, or clamps to pull the parts tight to each other as the glue sets.

LINE UP THE SIDES of the box in order and apply tape to hold the corners in alignment. Then spread glue on the mitered surfaces and assemble the box around the top panel and plywood bottom.

Drill for corner dowels

DOWELS ARE A GREAT WAY TO PROVIDE
mechanical strength to a glued miter joint. By offsetting the dowels slightly, they interlock, making
the corner nearly impossible to take apart. Dowels
are just as strong as nails and can add a touch of visible craftsmanship to the finished box. To be effective, however, the holes for the dowels need to be
carefully placed, which requires accurate measuring.
I place intersecting dowels at the top corners of the
lid, at the top corners of the body of the box, at the
mid-points of the box sides, and at the corners at
the back of the body of the box. Be aware that the
placement of the dowels should take into account
the points at which the lid will be cut from the body
of the box.

**I MAKE A SIMPLE SHOPMADE MARKING
GAUGE to mark the location of the dowel holes.
You can also just mark them with pencil and awl to be
ready to drill.**

USE THE DRILL PRESS to drill the dowel holes.

1. I use a pair of simple marking gauges made
from wood and nails (as shown above right) to
mark the box sides for the dowels. To ensure that
the dowels are symmetrical left and right, you
either need to make two of these opposite each
other or spend some time carefully measuring and

marking the location for each dowel. As is often
the case in my shop, I build more than one box at
a time, so it was worth taking the time to make a
device to mark the location of the holes to ensure
that they slightly overlap. With the jig in place, tap
each nail to make each mark. **(PHOTO A)** If you are
making only one box, very carefully measuring and
marking the dowel holes directly on the surface of
the box will suffice. Use a tape measure and awl to
mark the hole locations prior to drilling.

2. After marking the dowels holes, use the drill
press or power drill to drill them. **(PHOTO B)**

Carefully space corner dowels so
that they are offset from each other.
This will lock the miter in place.

Cut the lid from the body of the box

1. Set the height of the sawblade on the tablesaw so that it nearly passes through the thickness of the stock used in the box sides. Then set the fence so that what will remain of the sides of the box lid will equal 1 in. Hold the box on edge against the fence as you make the cut around the perimeter of the box, being careful that the blade doesn't cut all the way through as that would allow the lid to be pushed into the blade. **(PHOTO A)**

USE A SHARP KNIFE to finish the cut and liberate the lid from the body of the box.

CUT THE LID from the body of the box using the tablesaw. By leaving a bit of stock to be cut with a knife, I prevent the lid from being pressed into the sawblade at the finish of the cut.

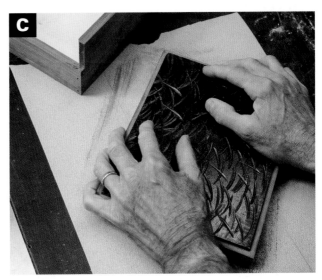

SAND THE SURFACES where the saw was used to cut the lid from the body of the box. I use adhesive-backed sandpaper on a flat surface as my sanding base.

2. Use a knife to test the cut. **(PHOTO B)** Perfect is when the knife passes through with just a bit of resistance.

3. Adhesive-backed sandpaper on a flat surface makes short work of smoothing out the underside of the lid and the top edges of the box after the lid is cut from the rest of the box. **(PHOTO C)**

Fit the hinges

ONCE THE LID IS CUT FROM THE BODY OF
the box, the lid and body can be routed on the
router table to form the hinge mortises. On a lid of
this type, getting the edges to align requires that the
hinge mortises be cut precisely. Butt hinges, when
housed by wood on three sides, are much easier to
align and the mortises provide exact locations. I use
my flipped story-stick technique to achieve perfect
alignment for the hinges. This technique ensures
that the hinge mortises on the lid align with the
hinge mortises on the body of the box, both left
and right.

MAKE A STORY STICK the exact same width as the
back of the box. With the tablesaw blade raised about
½ in. or so, cut away a spot for the hinge to fit.

1. Make a story stick the exact same length as
the back of the box. I like to make my story sticks
from scrap ⅛-in. birch plywood, as it is strong
and thin. While thicker wood can be used, I'll also
use this same story stick as a guide for installing a tab on the front of the lid. If it is too thick,
the router bit won't pass all the way through the
stock where its hole will be used when the stick
is flipped end for end to set up the stop block on
the other side. The more precise the story stick,
the more likely you can perform this operation
without extra chiseling or unwanted gaps.

2. Make cuts into the edge of the story stick
until one hinge will fit as shown. **(PHOTO A)** The
fit should be such that the hinge will fit in the cut
without being forced but will not fall out.

3. Set the height of the router bit above the
surface of the router table. Use a zero-clearance
insert in the router table to provide for accurate
measuring. For the solid brass Brusso® hinge used
in this box, the height needs to be just slightly
more than the thickness of one leaf of the hinge.
(PHOTO B)

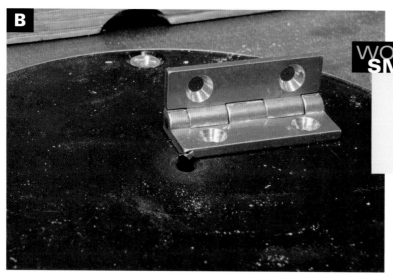

WORK SMART

A zero-clearance insert helps provide
for accurate measuring as it allows
you to put the hinge right up against
the bit to gauge the bit's height.

A ZERO-CLEARANCE ROUTER-TABLE
insert helps as you set the router bit height.
For this hinge, the height is set to just over
the thickness of one leaf.

SET THE DISTANCE of the bit from the fence by using the hinge as your guide. This controls how far your hinges will protrude into the back of the box.

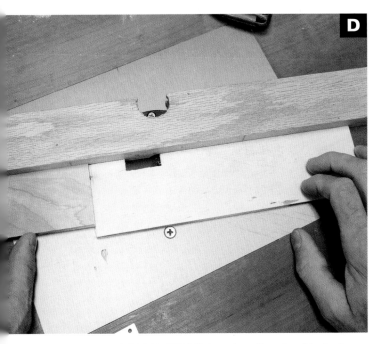

USE THE STORY STICK to set up the stop blocks to limit the area that the box and lid will travel over the router table. With the tips of the router bit oriented to the left and the right, slide the story stick to the left and right and clamp stop blocks against the story stick when it is at the widest range of its travel on both sides.

4. Setting the distance between the fence and the router bit will determine how far the hinge protrudes into the back edge of the box and lid; and different hinges have different requirements. On this Brusso hinge, the squared corners allow for a 90-degree stop when the box is open, and to avoid extra fitting, the full barrel must be exposed at the back of the box. Set the hinge in place to directly set the distance from the fence to the outer edge of the cut. **(PHOTO C)**

5. Use the story stick to locate the stop blocks that control the movement of the box and lid over the router table as you rout the hinge mortises. **(PHOTO D)** It will help to get a more accurate fit if you align the tips of the router bit to the left and right as you use the story stick. That way, the widest point in the cut will intersect the story stick during setup. Clamp the stop blocks firmly in place before routing the box.

6. After routing one side of the top and one side of the body of the box, remove the stop blocks and flip the story stick. It can now be used to determine the new location for the stop blocks. Clamp them in place and remember to align the router bit to its widest points left and right. **(PHOTO E)** You can finish the hinge mortises now by chiseling the corners square, or you can wait until the box is finished with Danish oil and ready for final assembly and hinge installation.

WHEN THE FIRST HINGE MORTISES are complete as shown, flip the story stick over to reset the stop blocks for the matching mortises.

USE THE SAME STORY STICK as your guide to rout the mortise for the lift tab on the lid of the box.

F

7. Using the same ⅛-in. router bit in the router table, rout a groove for the lid lift tab. I raise the height of the router bit to ³⁄₁₆ in. and use the story stick to determine the location for stop blocks to control the length of the groove. Just as the story stick was used to accurately set up the travel of the box lid and base on the router table, it can also be used to control the length of the groove and ensure that it is centered left and right on the front edge of the lid.

8. Set the distance from the fence to the router bit to equal the distance from the edge of the lid to the height at which you want to place your lift tab. (I set this at ⁵⁄₁₆ in.) Mark the location of one side of the tab on the story stick, lower it in place over the router bit so that it drills through while against the stop block on the right. (To make a groove for a ¾-in.-wide tab, make the hole ⅜ in. from the centerline.)

9. Then flip the story stick over, lower the hole over the router bit, and use the story stick as your guide for clamping the left stop block in place. **(PHOTO F)**

Install the dowels

A

CUT ⅛-IN. DOWELS to length and then tap them into place. Note that the dowel holes are offset from each other.

TO MAKE SMALL DOWELS OF UNIFORM length, I wrap about 10 dowels together with masking tape into a bundle so that several can be cut at the same time. I use the sled and stop block on the tablesaw to make the cuts. Then I gently round the ends with sandpaper so that they will be softer to the touch and will go into the holes more easily. All the sanding should be done on the outside of the box prior to installing the dowels. Tap in the small dowels to secure the corners. These need not be glued, as the friction fit will hold them forever. **(PHOTO A)**

Make the base

THE BASE OF THE BOX IS AN EASY MITERED assembly built around a piece of ⅛-in. Baltic-birch plywood. The plywood, glued in the corners of deep grooves, holds the parts together with lasting strength.

1. First, miter the parts. You will notice that once again the 2-in. spacer block comes into play as the ratio between the length and depth from front to back is still x:x +/-2 even though the base extends beyond all four sides. **(PHOTO A)**

2. Make a cut on the tablesaw into the edge of each mitered piece. The cut should be deep enough that the plywood panel gives the base strength where the parts are joined. **(PHOTO B)**

3. Measure the inside length of the tablesaw cuts to determine the size of the Baltic-birch plywood panel that will form the very bottom of the box.

4. Sand the inside edges of all the base parts as well as the plywood bottom before assembly. **(PHOTO C)** I also routed a small chamfer on each inside edge to give a more finished look.

5. During assembly, spread glue on the mitered surfaces and put a bit of extra glue into the grooves at the ends of the frame parts so that the Baltic-birch plywood panel becomes a structural component and makes other joinery methods unnecessary.

TO BEGIN MAKING the base, cut the basswood stock to length with the miter sled on the tablesaw. Use stop blocks to make sure the pairs of parts are exactly the same length.

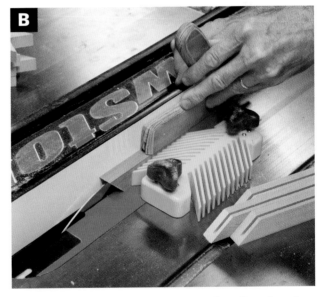

USE THE TABLESAW to make a cut into the edge of each base part.

SAND THE INSIDE edges of the base parts.

6. To give the base its final shape, after assembly adjust the tablesaw to cut a 30-degree angle from the edge of the base. To avoid cutting into the flat space needed for mounting the base to the box, set the fence so that the blade is ⅜ in. away from the fence. **(PHOTO D)**

7. After cutting the bottom to shape, use the angle grinder to apply texture to it just as you did the lid panel. Paint it to match that panel.

CUT THE BASE TO SHAPE on the tablesaw. Leave a flat space to mount the box base.

Make a drawer

MAKING DRAWERS TO FIT A BOX REQUIRES precise work. It's like making a box to fit precisely into another box. I've found it makes sense to first construct the outer box and then adjust the size of the inner box as necessary to fit. Don't try to make both at the same time and expect things to come out right. You may need to make adjustments to the size of the drawer after the body of the box is assembled. Refer back to the outer box to ascertain the correct part measurements. You should note that the drawer is intended to stand proud of the front of the body of the box, a total of ⅛ in.

1. I use a simple mortise-and-tenon technique to make small drawers, with both the mortise and tenon being formed on the router table. The mortise must be cut first so that the thickness of the tenon can be fine-tuned to fit. Put a ⅛-in. straight-cut router bit in the router table and set the fence so that the distance from the outside of the cut to the fence is only slightly greater than the thickness of the stock. This leaves just a small amount to be sanded flush following assembly.

2. Set up to rout the mortises at the ends of the two sides first. To make sure the mortise is the right length, use stops to control the travel of the workpiece across the router table. I set the stop blocks so that the mortise comes to about ³⁄₁₆ in.

TO FORM THE MORTISE for the drawer back to fit in the drawer sides, use a ⅛-in. straight router bit in the router table to rout ³⁄₁₆ in. deep. Use a dial caliper to check the depth.

MOVE THE DRAWER side from right to left between stops to make this routed groove. Because the drawer front extends over the sides, the mortises in it will need to be routed in a separate setup.

from the edges of the stock. A dial caliper helps to check depth, which should measure just slightly greater than $^3/_{16}$ in. **(PHOTO A)**

3. Hold the stock firmly against the stop block on the right and tight to the fence and then lower it over the spinning router bit. Keep the stock tight to the fence as you move it from right to left and back between stops. Then tilt it up from the cut. The mortise should be stopped on both ends so it will not be visible in the finished drawer. **(PHOTO B)**

4. To begin forming the tenons on the drawer sides and back, use a 1¼-in.-diameter straight bit in the router table with a ⅛-in. space between it and the router table fence. Raise its height to $^3/_{16}$ in. You will again find a dial caliper useful to make certain that the tenon length is exactly $^3/_{16}$ in. I use a zero-clearance insert in the router table to support the stock through the cut and use safety blocking to completely bury the cutter so that nothing but wood can come into contact with it. I use a safety cover over the router bit during this operation. It allows me to keep a good grip on

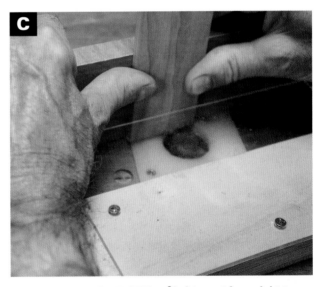

C

WITH THE HEIGHT SET at $^3/_{16}$ in., rout from right to left, keeping a very tight grip on the stock while holding it tight to the fence. Safety blocking or a clear Plexiglas shield as shown should be used to keep fingers a safe distance from the router bit.

the stock without putting my fingers at risk. Clamp the safety cover in place with just enough clearance so that the workpiece can pass safely through the cut. The stock must be held securely throughout the cut. **(PHOTO C)**

ROUT THE DRAWER SIDES and back to fit the drawer bottom. Stops on the router table are set up to control the cut so it doesn't go all the way through the mortises on the drawer sides. Stops are not required when routing the groove in the drawer back (shown here).

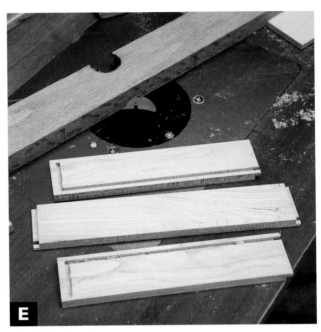

THESE ARE THE DRAWER SIDES and back with the grooves routed to fit the drawer bottom.

5. To cut the drawer parts to house the bottom panel, use a 1/8-in. straight-cut router bit set at a height of 1/8 in. with a space of 1/8 in. between it and the fence. **(PHOTO D)**

6. Use router-table stops to keep the cuts from moving all the way through the mortises at the ends of the drawer sides. To rout the back, remove the stops to rout clear through from one end to the other. The results are shown above right **(PHOTO E)**.

7. Change the setting of the router-table fence to locate the drawer-guide slots on the drawer sides. You'll find it easiest to determine the exact location of these guide slots by taking careful measurements from the bottom of the body of the box. **(PHOTO F)** Use scrap wood left over from forming the drawer parts to make test cuts. Observe the fit on your test pieces and make certain of your drawer alignment and clearance before you actually rout the drawer-guide grooves in the drawer sides.

8. After routing, move the fence about 1/32 in. farther away from the bit and rout again so that the

drawer guides to be fitted and glued to the inside of the box will slide smoothly on the drawer side. This makes the groove in the drawer sides slightly larger than the drawer guides and prevents the drawer guides from sticking.

ROUT THE GROOVES in the sides of the drawers to accommodate the drawer guides.

Make the drawer front

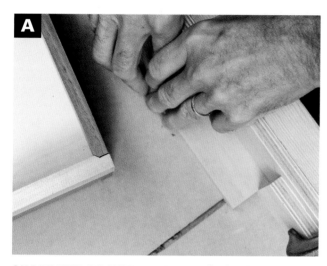

SHAPE THE DRAWER FRONT to fit the sides of the box as shown. This is done with two cuts. The first is on edge; the second forms the 45-degree cut using a stop block to position the cut.

1. The drawer front must first be fitted to the drawer sides as shown in the photo above **(PHOTO A)** . Cut the drawer front to size then shape it to fit the box sides. This requires two cuts on each end, one to form the flat surface and a second completed on the tablesaw with the blade tilted to 45 degrees using the tablesaw miter sled. Use a stop block to control the position of the cut. You may want to start with the blade lower than required and work your way up to a perfect fit in small increments to avoid cutting too deep.

2. Once the drawer front is shaped, it can be carved with the angle grinder, making marks similar to those formed on the top panel and base. Then use spray paint or milk paint and let dry.

BECAUSE THE DRAWER SIDES are not as tall as the drawer front, routing for the bottom to fit the drawer front requires a separate setup with the bit $\frac{1}{32}$ in. farther from the fence. Rout between stops with the bit entering the mortises formed on each end.

3. To rout the drawer front for the sides, use the same technique as for routing mortises in the drawer sides. You will need to carefully set the distance between the fence and the router table cut, and again set the depth to slightly over $\frac{3}{16}$ in.

4. Rout the drawer front for the drawer bottom to fit. For this, lower the height of the router bit to $\frac{1}{8}$ in. This requires careful measuring. Make certain the sides and bottom fit the drawer front in just the right place, with the height of the drawer front centered on the drawer sides with proper clearance between the base of the box and the underside of the box front. **(PHOTO B)** You will note that the drawer front is taller than the drawer sides to provide greater clearance on opening. Also note that the drawer front is slightly smaller in height than the opening allowed for it.

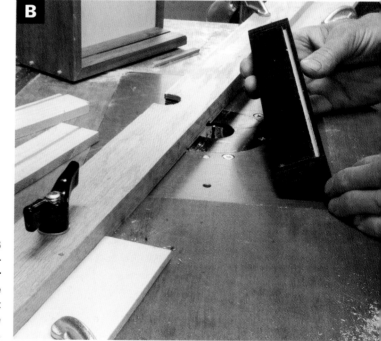

Assemble the drawer

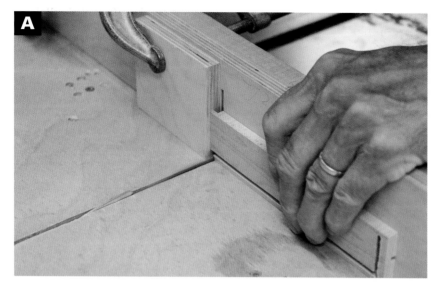

TRIM THE TENONS at the top and bottom of each part of the drawer to fit the mortises routed in the sides and front.

USE A SQUEEZE bottle to apply glue to the insides of each mortise as the drawer is assembled.

1. In order for the tenons on the drawer sides to fit the drawer fronts, they must be trimmed to width using the cross-cut sled and stop block on the tablesaw as shown. **(PHOTO A)**

2. When you are ready to assemble all the drawer parts, first sand them, as you will get no chance to do so effectively after the parts are glued together.

3. To make certain assembly will go smoothly after glue is applied, do a trial fit with the drawer bottom in place. When ready, use a squeeze bottle to put a dab of glue inside the mortises as you assemble the drawer. **(PHOTO B)** If your parts are well fitted, clamping may be unnecessary, but have rubber bands or tape ready to make certain parts are held in alignment, and be certain to check that the drawer assembly is square.

4. After the drawer is assembled, use a ⅛-in. router bit to rout a groove on the front for a pull to fit, just as you did in routing a groove for the lift tab on the lid.

Attach the base

I USE SCREWS TO ATTACH THE BASE TO
the rest of the box. Careful measuring is required.

1. To start you'll need to locate your first screw on the base of the box. Measure 5¼ in. from each end at the underside of the back of the base, and mark with an awl exactly ¹¹⁄₁₆ in. from the edge. Then drill with a countersink bit deep enough for the head of the screw to be flush.

2. You need to locate where that first screw from the base of the box will attach to the body of the box. Measure to the halfway point along the bottom edge at the back of the body of the box and make a mark with the awl centered at the edge of the stock. Drill just deep enough for the screw to get a good grip without splitting the wood. This will be about ⅜ in. deep.

3. Once you've drilled the hole in the base and the corresponding hole in the body of the box, place the bottom in position and put the screw through the hole in the base and guide it carefully into position on the back edge of the body of the box. Once this screw has been tightened, holding the base to the body of the box, adjust the position of the base so the remaining screws can be countersunk and driven into the box. **(PHOTO A)** Each of the screws should be located ¹¹⁄₁₆ in. from the edge of the base.

USE SCREWS TO ATTACH the base to the underside of the box. Put the screw in the center at the back first and then adjust the position of the sides so that an equal amount of space is shown on all sides.

Make dividers

A

TO MAKE DIVIDERS for the top compartment of the box, make cuts while sliding the parts between two stop blocks. A small amount of extra space between the stop blocks allows the saw cut to be widened to fit the thickness of the stock used.

MAKE YOUR DIVIDERS with two different widths of stock and the lap joint will be hidden, as long as your cuts are made accurately.

B

IT IS EASY TO MAKE DIVIDERS TO FIT INSIDE this box. On the tablesaw, I make half-lap joints to connect the parts by using a sled and stop blocks to control the position of the cuts.

1. Mill the stock to a uniform thickness, then cut the parts to length to fit front-to-back and side-to-side on the inside of the box. In order for this technique to work, the parts must be cut to uniform length. To ensure this, use the sled and stop block.

2. To form the lap cuts in matching parts, I use two stop blocks, one on the left and one on the right. By using two stop blocks, the width of the

cut can be widened to fit various thicknesses of stock by sliding the stock from one stop block to the other. Make your first cut against one stop block and then slide it to the other to widen the cut. **(PHOTO A)**

3. I always make extra stock so that I can fine-tune the fit as I adjust the positions of the two stop blocks. Also, by using two different widths of stock, one size running from front-to-back and the other side-to-side, the joints are effectively hidden from view. **(PHOTO B)** This works because the differing heights hide the joint between them, as shown above.

Color with Milk Paints

YOU CAN USE LAYERED MILK PAINTS TO add interest to a textured box. If you paint one layer over another and then sand through, it gives the appearance of an antique finish, accentuating the use of texture.

1. First, apply one color to the textured wood. **(PHOTO A)**

2. A second color applied after the first has dried goes into the textured areas where even heavy sanding can't reach. **(PHOTO B)**

(ABOVE) YOU CAN HIGHLIGHT TEXTURE through the use of milk paints. Milk paints, unlike most, can be easily sanded and layered. Paint a base coat with one color and let it dry.

(RIGHT) WHEN THE BASE COLOR is dry, apply a second coat using another color.

AFTER BOTH COLORS are dry, use fine sandpaper, steel wool, or a Scotch-Brite™ pad to sand through parts of the top layer, revealing the other colors underneath.

3. Through sanding and by layering various colors on textured woods, interesting combinations of texture and color can create attractive effects. **(PHOTO C)**

Make a Dovetailed Variation

THE DOWELED MITER MIGHT actually be more texture than you'd like. In that case, you can use other joinery techniques to make this same box. On one variation, I used mitered hand-cut dovetails but a keyed miter joint would also work.

1. Use a marking gauge to scribe lines to guide the chisel in forming the dovetailed joints. The gauge should be set so that it is slightly wider than the thickness of the stock. **(PHOTO A)**

FOR THE MORE ADVENTUROUS and experienced craftsman, a mitered hand-cut dovetail is an alternate method of making the jewelry box.

USE A MARKING GAUGE to scribe a line on both sides of each piece. Set the distance on the marking gauge to be slightly greater than the thickness of the stock.

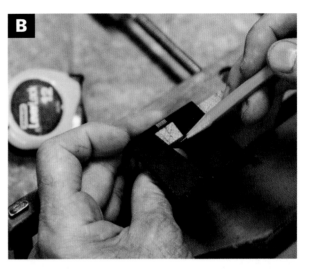

CAREFULLY LAY OUT the position for each pin. You will need to make sure that you allow for the sawcut separating the lid from the body of the box.

CONTINUE THE MARKS on the face of the stock.

USE A DOVETAIL SAW or dozuki saw to cut the pins for the dovetail joint.

2. Mark the location of the pins using a dovetail marking template or sliding T bevel. **(PHOTO B)**

3. Finish marking the pins using a square. **(PHOTO C)**

4. Saw the pins but leave the last one sawn at a 45-degree angle from the tip of the outside corner to the marking gauge line (to allow the joint to be finished on the tablesaw). **(PHOTO D)**

5. Remove the waste between the pins using a bandsaw, scrollsaw, or coping saw. **(PHOTO E)**

6. Use a chisel to remove the waste between the pins. Make your first cuts slightly away from the marking gauge line, and then when you make your

final cuts with the chisel right on the line, they will be crisp and clean. **(PHOTO F)**

7. Use the tablesaw and miter gauge set at 45 degrees to finish the miter at the top edge of the box. This cut will allow you to accurately mark the dovetails on the adjoining stock. **(PHOTO G)**

USE A BANDSAW or coping saw to remove waste from between the pins to reduce the amount of chiseling that will be required.

USE A CHISEL to remove the waste, cutting up to the marking gauge lines on both sides.

ONCE THE PINS have been formed, make the miter cuts at the top corners of the front and back of the box.

USE THE FRONT and back to directly mark the locations of the pins on the box ends. Use a sharp knife for the best results in marking from one to the other.

USE A DOVETAIL saw or dozuki saw to remove the waste and form the dovetails to match the pins. All that remains on this joint is to cut the final miter on the box end, which allows the parts to fit.

8. Trace the pins directly onto the adjoining stock to determine the location of the dovetails. **(PHOTO H)** I clamp a piece of wood along the marking gauge line on the dovetail side, so that the already-cut piece can be held tightly in position as the pins are traced with a knife.

9. When the dovetails are cut, all that remains will be to miter the top corners of the dovetailed sides. **(PHOTO I)**

10. Go back to the tablesaw for a few more small cuts using the miter gauge set at 45 degrees. **(PHOTO J)**

11. You will need to change the angle to cut 45 degrees on the opposite side to finish the joints so that all four corners fit as shown. **(PHOTO K)**

RETURN TO THE TABLESAW to make the final cuts. A simple jig mounted to the tablesaw miter guide can be fine-tuned to make the final mitered cuts.

THE DOVETAIL GIVES A REFINED LOOK that speaks of quality, but it takes practice.

Carve a Jewelry Box

YET ANOTHER variation of this box as an exploration of texture is to carve a deliberate pattern, like this one of dogwood blossoms carved on a basswood box. I used a paper template to lay out the dogwood blossom locations and then sketched in the leaves and stems. Cut the outline of each element using a small straight chisel, and then use a shallow gouge to remove the background. **(PHOTO A)**

TEXTURE CAN ALSO BE APPLIED in a less random manner through simple relief carving, as in this basswood variation using a dogwood motif.

A Magnetic Tower
of Boxes

IN MAKING THIS TOWER
of boxes, we'll explore the
use of balance and symmetry.
Balance and symmetry are important concerns in three-dimensional
design, and this box consisting
of magnetically connected layers
neatly fits our innate desire for
order despite what might seem to
be an insecure means of attachment. The lid and base are the
exact same shape and dimension
but are mirror images of each other.
With rare earth magnets, the tower
of boxes can be built as tall or as
short as you like using design skills
and techniques learned earlier in
this book. A single box and lid with
a detachable base, secured by
rare earth magnets, makes a nice
small box with a hidden compartment while as many as six or seven
boxes makes a nice stack.

Rare earth magnets have an
incredible holding power. They are
able to connect the various layers
of this box securely to each other
yet still allow the layers to be
taken apart to gain access to the
storage inside.

Magnetic tower of boxes

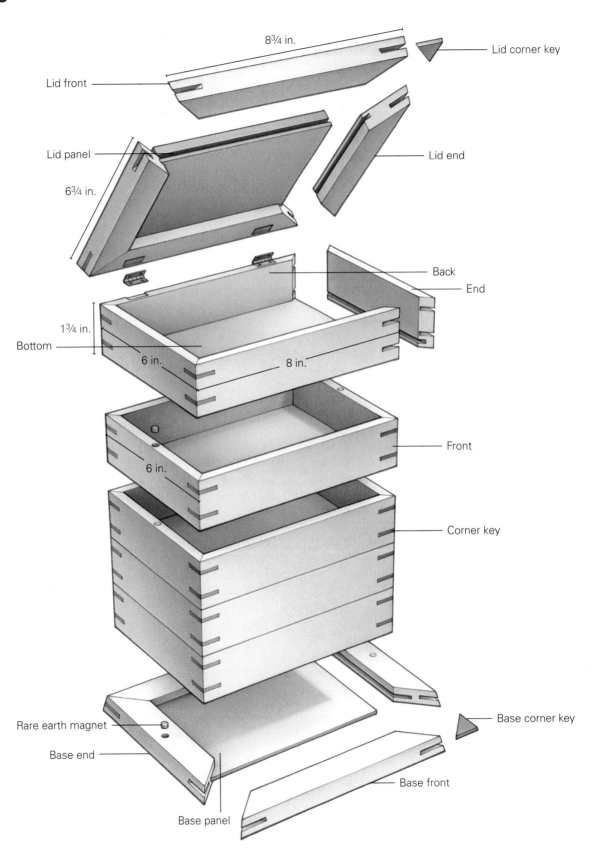

8¾ in.

Lid corner key

Lid front

Lid panel

Lid end

6¾ in.

Back

End

1¾ in.

Bottom

6 in.

8 in.

Front

6 in.

Corner key

Rare earth magnet

Base corner key

Base end

Base front

Base panel

QUANTITY	PART	MATERIAL	SIZE	NOTES
10	Front and back	Sycamore	$3/8$ in. x $1\,3/4$ in. x 8 in.	
10	End pieces	Sycamore	$3/8$ in. x $1\,3/4$ in. x 6 in.	
5	Bottom	Baltic-birch plywood	$1/8$ in. x $5\,5/8$ in. x $7\,5/8$ in.	
40	Corner keys	Walnut	$1/8$ in. x $11/16$ in. x $11/16$ in.	Triangles cut from $1/8$-in. x $5/8$-in. walnut stock
4	Lid and base front and back	Sycamore	$5/8$ in. x $1\,1/4$ in. x $8\,3/4$ in.	
4	Lid and base ends	Sycamore	$5/8$ in. x $1\,1/4$ in. x $6\,3/4$ in.	
1	Lid panel	Walnut	$9/16$ in. x $4\,5/8$ in. x $6\,5/8$ in.	
1	Base panel	Baltic-birch plywood	$1/8$ in. x $5\,1/4$ in. x $7\,1/4$ in.	
8	Lid and base corner keys	Walnut	$1/8$ in. x $7/8$ in. x $7/8$ in	Triangles cut from $1/8$-in. x $7/8$-in. walnut stock
18	Rare earth magnets		$1/4$ in. diameter x $1/8$ in. thick	www.kjmagnetics.com part number D42-N52
1 pair	Brass hinges	Narrow butt hinges	1 in. x $3/4$ in.	Ace Hardware number 5299730
1	Ball-chain lid support	3-in. number 3 ball chain and connectors		www.LeeValley.com stock number 00G48.01 for 6 sets

The layered compartments of this complex box are made in the same manner as the Lift-Lid Rectangular Box. Making the lid and base is similar to making the lid and base for the Finger-Jointed Chest. The technique for installing the hinges is more complicated than in earlier boxes in that it requires a double story stick, which I'll show you how to make. The precise installation of the magnets requires many of the skills of measuring and construction that you've developed through making other boxes in this book.

While the main box featured in this chapter is intended to illustrate balance and perfect symmetry as each layer stacks neatly and securely on the preceding layer, every principle or element of design has its corresponding opposite. Just as one person might be drawn to symmetry, there are others who are drawn to spontaneity and chaos. At the close of this chapter, this principle of balance and order vs. asymmetry and chaos is tested in a box, the layers of which you can arrange unevenly, thus pushing the limits of balance and your own comfort with chaos.

Balance and Symmetry

BALANCE AND SYMMETRY ARE IMPORTANT
to consider when designing in 3-D. Things that
look as though they are physically off-balance and
likely to fall over may make the viewer uncom-
fortable. In addition to physical balance, objects
and components of objects have what artists call
"visual weight," meaning that they give an illusion
of heaviness or lightness, although that may not
actually be the case. For instance, ornamentation
on one side of a box may make that side appear
heavier or lighter relative to the other side of the
box. Feet may create a space at the underside of
a box, making the box appear lighter. A base, on
the other hand, may make a box feel more firmly
rooted and secure on the surface it rests on. The
shape of box sides, as shown in the alternate
design on p. 71, can make a box feel more firmly
rooted to the earth. Imagine the same box upside
down, and you can easily see that it would appear
unsteady on its feet, and liable to topple. Visual weight
is a very real concern that you should keep in mind
when designing your boxes.

Many boxmakers, in their quest for beauty, will look
to symmetry as a means to achieve balance. In other
words, what we do to one side must be done to the
other. When using this strategy, pulls and lift tabs must
be exactly centered to provide a sense of balance and
symmetry on both sides. Where symmetry connects
one side to another and similar design elements are
used to create a sense of balance, the viewer will see
the maker's underlying intentions; that the beautiful
box was not just happenstance, but was the result of
deliberation and care.

The use of balance and symmetry offers a conserva-
tive point of view in boxmaking, which might run the
risk of boring the viewer. Instead, you could take a
more playful and risky approach. Deliberately avoiding
perfect balance may present greater risk but can pay

CENTERING PARTICULAR FEATURES like these
knots on both the lid and the body of a box illustrates
balance and symmetry.

off in big rewards by turning a somewhat conserva-
tive object into a more expressive work of art. Playing
with these concepts rather than simply accepting them
as a rule offers surprising and engaging results. For
instance, the maple box at the close of this chapter can
be arranged to appear off-balance or to have a sense of
spiral movement that takes it far beyond the ordinary.

While perfect balance and symmetry can be used
to create a pleasing, yet potentially static object, less
than perfect balance or asymmetry may create a sense
of movement. In any case, consideration of balance
and symmetry and its alternatives provides a useful
lens through which to critique our own work and to
consider how we might make our designs more interesting and beautiful.

Prepare the stock

THIS BOX REQUIRES THAT MATERIAL BE
resawn and planed to 3⁄8 in. thick. Sections of the
stock 29 in. to 30 in. long will be enough to form
the parts of each layer with the grain matched at
three corners. Mark the various parts when they
are cut. You will find it helpful to sand the inside
surfaces of each strip of wood before it is cut
to length.

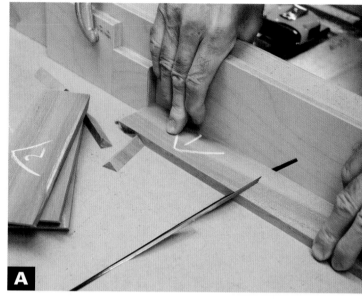

A

USE THE MITER SLED on the tablesaw to cut the
parts to length. A 2-in. spacer block is used to alternate
cut lengths.

Cut the parts and assemble the boxes

1. Use the miter sled on the tablesaw to cut the
parts to length. I use a 2-in. spacer block between
cuts to get the two different board lengths needed
to form the rectangular-shaped boxes. Cut and
carefully mark and group the pieces for reassembly. **(PHOTO A)**

2. On the tablesaw cut the grooves in the side
pieces for the bottom to fit. **(PHOTO B)** I set the
fence 3⁄16 in. from the blade so that the bottom will
fit that distance from the edge of the stock. This
distance is to allow for the 1⁄8-in.-thick rare earth
magnets that will be used to connect the boxes
in a stack.

CUT A GROOVE
along the inside of
each piece for the
bottoms to fit.

B

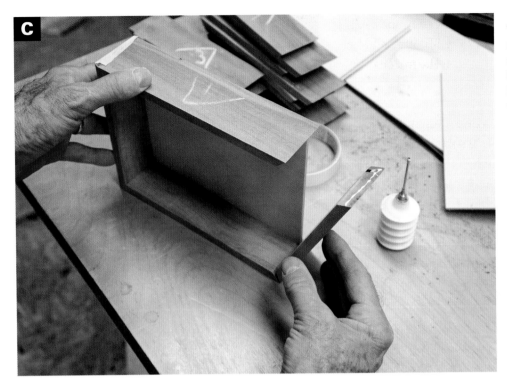

C

TAPE THREE CORNERS together and then assemble the boxes around the box bottoms using glue on each mitered surface.

3. Cut the Baltic-birch plywood bottoms to fit and sand them smooth prior to assembly. I always do a test fit before I get out the glue to make sure that everything will go together with ease. Use tape to hold the parts together at three corners, apply glue to the mitered surfaces, and then roll the sides around the bottom of the box. **(PHOTO C)** Use rubber bands to hold the parts together as the glue sets and make certain that the edges are aligned before you set the box aside for the glue to dry.

Install the miter keys

A

1. Flatten the top and bottom of the boxes with self-adhesive sandpaper mounted on a flat surface. **(PHOTO A)**

2. Use a keyed miter guide (see p. 30) to cut the grooves in the corners of the boxes for the contrasting walnut keys. A spacer block laid in the

USE SELF-ADHESIVE SANDPAPER on a flat surface to sand the top and bottom of the boxes to make certain that the edges are aligned.

body of the jig provides a secure location for each cut. **(PHOTO B)** The height of the blade should be carefully set so it does not cut into the inside of the box.

3. Cut triangular keys of walnut and glue them into the corners of each box. Then, after the glue has dried, carefully sand each side flat. You can do this either on the flat sanding sheet by hand or on the stationary belt sander.

Drill for the magnets to fit

INSTALLING THE MAGNETS TO HOLD THE parts of the box together requires careful measuring and the use of a drill press to make absolutely certain the parts of the box are aligned.

1. Use a fence on the drill press so that you can position the drill to go at the center of the ³⁄₈-in.-thick stock, and use stop blocks on both sides so that the box will be held exactly in position as the holes are drilled. **(PHOTO A)** Adjust the depth stop on the drill so that the hole depth is the precise thickness of the magnets used, ¹⁄₈ in.

WORK SMART

Don't install the magnets until you are ready for final assembly as they can be difficult or impossible to remove, and if you get any of them reversed they can repel instead of attract.

CUT KEYED MITER slots on the tablesaw. A spacer block is used in the keyed miter guide to hold the box in the right position for each cut.

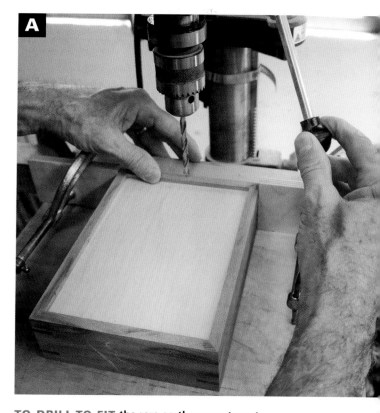

TO DRILL TO FIT the rare earth magnets, set up the drill press with a fence in position so that the tip of the ¼-in. drill falls at the center of the ³⁄₈-in. stock. Set up stop blocks on the left and right to position the box so that the drill will hit dead center from each side.

SET THE DEPTH of the drill to drill ⅛ in. deep so that the magnets will install flush with the surface. Drill at each end of the box. Next, drill matching holes at the underside of each end of the box. The top box should be drilled only on the underside.

2. Drill at each end, then turn the box over and drill matching holes on the other side. **(PHOTO B)** If these holes are not centered, the boxes will not stack in exact relationship to each other, so take great care in setting up the stop blocks.

Note that no holes for magnets are required on the top edges of the top layer, as this layer will have a hinged lid instead.

Make the lid and base

USE THE MITER sled to make a frame for the lid and base. Again, the 2-in. spacer block is used to alter the distance between the stop block and the line of cut to form a rectangular structure, matching the proportions of the box.

1. Prepare stock ⅝ in. thick, 1¼ in. wide, and about 32 in. long for the lid frame and an equal piece for the base frame. Use the miter sled on the tablesaw to cut the parts to length. Just as in making the box front, back, and ends, the 2-in. spacer block allows for cutting alternating lengths from a single piece of stock. **(PHOTO A)**

2. Cut the panels to length first and then put the spacer block against the stop block to cut the panels to width. **(PHOTO B)** Cut the top panel slightly narrower (1/32 in.) to allow for possible expansion.

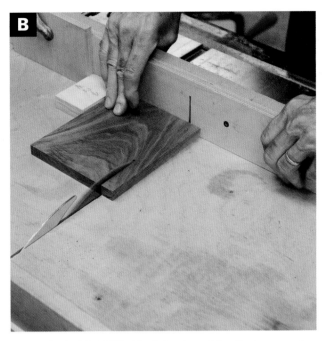

WITH THE SPACER block in place, trim the top panel to the required dimension.

MAKE TEST CUTS to prepare the saw for shaping the top panel and lid sides to fit. A simple interlocking joint as shown is required, both parts made with a single setup of the saw. Set the blade height at $3/16$ in. and the distance between the blade and fence exactly equal to the width of the sawkerf.

3. Fitting the top panel to the lid frame takes a careful setup on the tablesaw. Set the blade height at $3/16$ in. and the opening between the fence and blade equal to the width of the sawkerf. Make test cuts on scrap wood until you have adjusted the fence location for a perfect fit. (PHOTO **C**) The test parts should slide together easily but without visible gaps.

4. Use the setting you've just established to cut the edges of the lid frame and the edges of the top panel as shown. (PHOTO **D**) I chose to cut the base frame and Baltic-birch plywood panel in a separate operation so that I could make the Baltic-birch piece larger to serve as a structural component in the finished box. For the base frame, I set the fence so that the blade cut $3/16$ in. from the edge of the

CUT THE GROOVES in the lid frame parts and then make a matching cut along each edge of the top panel.

SPREAD GLUE ON the mitered surfaces (but not in the groove) and assemble the frame around the top panel

stock, with the blade height at ½ in. I sized the Baltic-birch panel to fit the dimensions in the materials list.

5. To assemble the lid frame and base frame, spread glue on the mitered surfaces. Since the lid has a floating panel, avoid putting glue in the groove where the panel will fit. **(PHOTO E)**

6. On the base frame, I take the opposite approach and deliberately put a small amount of glue in the grooves where the corners meet so that the Baltic-birch plywood base panel will strengthen the joints. If you have tightly fitting miters, large rubber bands will apply sufficient pressure to hold the parts in alignment as the glue sets. **(PHOTO F)**

7. Use the tablesaw to cut the slots for the walnut keys in the edges of the assembled lid and base. **(PHOTO G)** While the miter keys are not required to strengthen the corner joints in the base (the plywood does that), I used the contrasting keys to provide visual balance and symmetry with the lid. The blade height should be set at about ¾ in. high for this cut.

USE LARGE RUBBER bands to hold the parts of the lid tightly around the top panel as the glue sets.

MAKE CUTS INTO the corners of the lid and base for the contrasting walnut keys to fit.

AFTER RIPPING the walnut key stock to dimension, bundle strips together before cutting them on the table-saw. Cutting small bundles of triangles keeps them from being thrown by the saw, and the triangular shape makes them easier to sand flush with the surrounding stock.

8. Make the key stock ⅛ in. thick and ⅞ in. wide. Wrap several pieces in a bundle so that they can be safely cut on the tablesaw using the miter sled. **(PHOTO H)** Glue a walnut key in each slot.

9. Attaching the base to the stack of boxes will require additional magnets. Carefully measure and mark the locations for the magnets. Then adjust the fence and depth of the drill. **(PHOTO I)** I determined the location for the holes by care-fully measuring the distance between the holes on the bottoms of the boxes and then marking the base to make sure that the intended holes would be the same distance apart. Drill to an exact depth of ⅛ in.

10. Use the tablesaw with the blade tilted to 15 degrees to shape the lid and base. I adjusted the distance from the fence to the blade so that only a ⅛-in.-wide flat surface would be left fol-lowing the cut. **(PHOTO J)** This way, the same amount would be removed from each side. Cutting the same shape on the ends requires a second setting of the fence.

DRILL HOLES FOR the magnets to fit into the base.

WITH THE TABLESAW blade tilted to 15 degrees, trim the edges of the top and bottom. Set the distance between the fence and blade so that a small flat edge is left on each side.

Install the hinges

THIS BOX IS MADE WITH THE LID OVER-
hanging the base, a design option that eliminates
the need for a pull and also adds flair to the box.
The design does offer some additional complication
in that a conventional story stick as used in earlier
chapters won't work. So I use a two-part story stick
that allows me to exactly reference the hinge mortises on the box to the hinge mortises on the lid.

1. To make this more complicated story stick,
first cut the stick the same length as the lid.
Then notch the corners on one edge so that the
length of that side is equal in length to the body
of the box. **(PHOTO A)**

2. After cutting the two sides of the story stick
to represent the two lengths, use the tablesaw to
cut out the space representing the width of the
hinge. **(PHOTO B)** If the hinge fits exactly in the
space cut, it will fit exactly in the space cut on
the router table when the setup is made using the
stick. You will note in the photo below that I have
two stop blocks set up on the sled, providing a
starting and stopping point for cutting the hinge
recess. Use those same start and stop points for
cutting an exact duplicate of the hinge recess on
the other side. They will also be used to set up the
router table to rout the hinge mortises in the lid.

3. Set up the router table. First set the height of
the router bit to cut to a depth almost one-half
the thickness of the barrel of the hinge. Then set
up the distance from the fence so that part or all
of the barrel will protrude from the back of the
box. **(PHOTO C)** For this operation, installing a

A

MAKE A TWO-SIDED STORY STICK to adjust for
the lid overhanging the body of the box. Cut the story
stick to the length of the lid, and then on one side trim
from each end until it is the length of the body of the box.

USE STOP BLOCKS on both sides
of the cut to form the space for the
hinge. When you get a perfect fit on
one edge as shown, do the same operation on the other side.

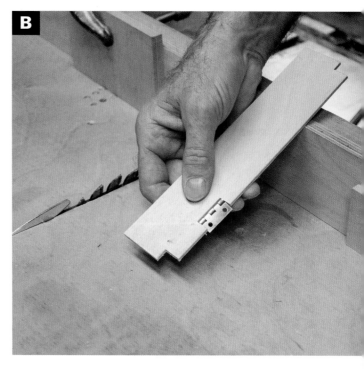

B

lid that overhangs the front, back, and sides of the box, I use a spacer strip to cover the fence, in effect, narrowing the distance between the fence and the cut. Because the lid overhangs the back of the box by ⅜ in., I use a ⅜-in.-thick spacer strip that will be removed when it is time to rout the hinge mortises in the lid.

4. Use the short side of the story stick to set up the stop blocks to rout the hinge mortises in the back edge of the body of the box. **(PHOTO D)**

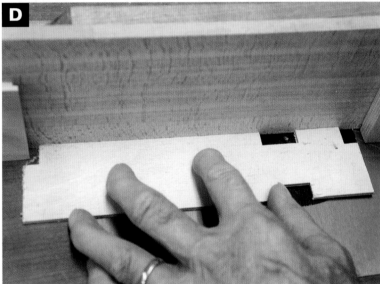

5. Rout one side and then flip the story stick end for end and use it to set up the stop blocks to rout the matching mortise on the other side. **(PHOTO E)**

(TOP) SET THE HEIGHT of the ⅛-in. router bit to equal just less than one-half the thickness of the hinge. Set the fence so that the barrel of the hinge will extend beyond the edge of the back of the body of the box. Use a ⅜-in. spacer strip on the router table fence to allow for the overhang of the lid at the back of the box.

(MIDDLE) USE THE STORY STICK to position the stop blocks and control the travel of the box on the router table.

(BOTTOM) ROUT ONE SIDE of the body of the box to fit the hinge, then flip the story stick end for end and use it to set up the stop blocks to rout the other side.

F

REMOVE THE SPACER strip from the fence and then use the longer side of the story stick to set up the stop blocks for routing the hinge mortises in the lid. To keep the hinge housed on four sides, use an additional fence clamped to the router table.

6. Remove the spacer strip from the router table fence. This will allow the router bit to cut farther in from the edge of the lid—by 3/8 in., the depth of the overhang at the back of the box. Use the longer portion of the story stick to set up the stop blocks to rout the lid. **(PHOTO F)**

7. I use a second fence clamped to the surface of the router table and parallel to the main fence to control the position of the lid from four sides. This gives the hinge a rectangular place to nest in the lid of the box and also decreases the visibility of the hinge in the finished box. **(PHOTO G)**

G

THE SECOND FENCE on the router table (as shown in photo F) allows the mortise to be cut as shown here so the hinge is fully housed on all four sides.

Install the magnets

AFTER SANDING AND FINISHING THE BOX, install the magnets. Be aware that this step is very easy to mess up. I've done it, and this is what I've learned from that experience.

1. Arrange the rare earth magnets in a tall stack and mark one end with an indelible marker. Working from just one end of the stack, apply super glue in each hole and slide a magnet from the stack into each hole at the top of each box, all the while being certain that the marked end of the stack of magnets is clearly in sight. **(PHOTO A)**

2. When all the magnets are installed in the top edges of the layers, and also in the base, you will be ready to glue the magnets into the underside of each layer. To install these magnets, all the while keeping the polarity between them so that they attract, mark the other end of the stack of magnets in another color. Proceed to install the magnets into the holes, again making sure that the newly marked end is always in sight. The magnets will be in the right relationship to each other to attract and not repel.

COLLECT THE MAGNETS in a tall stack and mark one end with color to help keep track of polarity. Install in all the top edges. When installing the magnets in the bottom, work from the other end of the stack. Again, marking the end of the stack of magnets will help you to keep track.

Scale It Up or Down

THE TOWER OF BOXES CAN BE MADE
in different sizes and designs. For instance,
this sycamore and walnut box, made to a
much smaller size, requires smaller magnets
and has a lift-off lid. Like the larger version,
the base is also held on by magnets. I routed
a small secret compartment in it just as was
done in the alternate project on p. 34.

BOX TOWERS CAN be made in
a range of sizes and with lift-off lids.

MATERIALS

QUANTITY	PART	MATERIAL	SIZE	NOTES
8	Front and back	Sycamore	$3/8$ in. x 2 in. x 5 in.	
8	End pieces	Sycamore	$3/8$ in. x 2 in. x 3 in.	
4	Bottom	Baltic-birch plywood	$1/8$ in. x $2^{5}/8$ in. x $4^{5}/8$ in.	
32	Corner keys	Walnut	$1/8$ in. x $^{11}/_{16}$ in. x $^{11}/_{16}$ in.	Triangles cut from $1/8$-in. x $5/8$-in. walnut stock
1	Lid	Walnut	$5/8$ in. x $3^{1}/2$ in. x $5^{1}/2$ in.	
1	Base	Walnut	$5/8$ in. x $3^{1}/2$ in. x $5^{1}/2$ in.	
14	Rare earth magnets		$3/16$ in. diameter x $1/8$ in. thick	www.kjmagnetics.com part number D32-N52

A Twisting Maple Tower

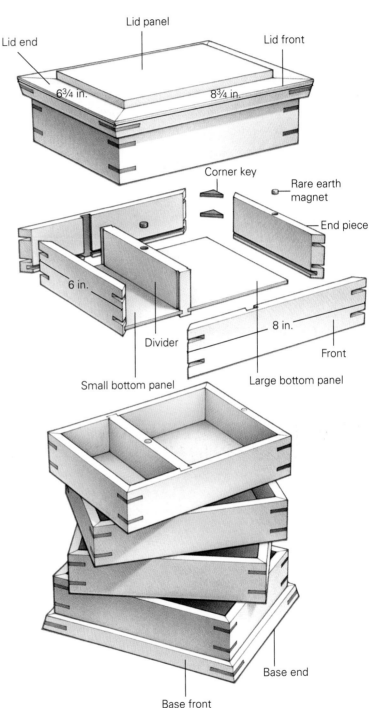

Lid panel

Lid end

Lid front

6¾ in.

8¾ in.

Corner key

Rare earth magnet

End piece

6 in.

Divider

8 in.

Front

Small bottom panel

Large bottom panel

Base end

Base front

JUST AS BALANCE AND SYMMETRY can be useful design goals, asymmetry and imbalance can add great interest to a box. By installing a divider in each layer of the box and installing the magnets in holes drilled in the top and bottom of the divider, the various layers can be rotated out of alignment with each other (or turned into balance) upon the whim of the owner.

1. To install a divider, rout a space for the divider in the front and back parts. I chose to use a sliding dovetail to hold the divider in place. **(PHOTO A, p. 163)** I put a dovetail bit in the router table and set the distance from the center of the bit to the fence at 2¾ in. Group your parts for routing so that they represent mirror sides. I use a push block to hold the parts square as they go through the cut.

MATERIALS

QTY	PART	MATERIAL	SIZE	NOTES
12	Front and back	Maple	$\frac{3}{8}$ in. x 2 in. x 8 in.	
12	Ends	Maple	$\frac{3}{8}$ in. x 2 in. x 6 in.	
6	Dividers	Maple	$\frac{1}{2}$ in. x 2 in. x $4\frac{5}{8}$ in.	
6	Large bottom panels	Baltic-birch plywood	$\frac{1}{8}$ in. x $4\frac{1}{2}$ in. x $4\frac{13}{16}$ in.	
6	Small bottom panels	Baltic-birch plywood	$\frac{1}{8}$ in. x $4\frac{1}{2}$ in. x $2\frac{9}{16}$ in.	
48	Corner keys	Walnut	$\frac{1}{8}$ in. x $\frac{11}{16}$ in. x $\frac{11}{16}$ in.	Triangles cut from $\frac{1}{8}$-in. x $\frac{5}{8}$-in. walnut stock
4	Lid and base front and back	Maple	$\frac{5}{8}$ in. x $1\frac{1}{4}$ in. x $8\frac{3}{4}$ in.	
4	Lid and base ends	Maple	$\frac{5}{8}$ in. x $1\frac{1}{4}$ in. x $6\frac{3}{4}$ in.	
1	Lid panel	Maple	$\frac{9}{16}$ in. x $4\frac{5}{8}$ in. x $6\frac{5}{8}$ in.	
1	Base panel	Baltic-birch plywood	$\frac{1}{8}$ in. x $5\frac{1}{4}$ in. x $7\frac{1}{4}$ in.	
8	Corner keys	Walnut	$\frac{1}{8}$ in. x $\frac{7}{8}$ in. x $\frac{7}{8}$ in	Triangles cut from $\frac{1}{8}$-in. x $\frac{7}{8}$-in.-walnut stock
4	Rare earth magnets		$\frac{1}{4}$ in. diameter x $\frac{1}{8}$ in. thick	www.kjmagnetics.com Part number D42-N52
10	Rare earth magnets		$\frac{5}{16}$ in. diameter x $\frac{1}{8}$ in. thick	www.kjmagnetics.com Part number D52-N52
10	Rare earth magnets		$\frac{1}{8}$ in. diameter x $\frac{3}{16}$ in. thick	www.kjmagnetics.com Part number D32-N52
1 pair	Brass hinges	Narrow butt hinges	1 in. x $\frac{3}{4}$ in.	Ace Hardware number 5299730
1	Ball-chain lid support	3-in. number 3 ball chain and connectors		www.LeeValley.com stock number 00G48.01 for 6 sets

2. Form the same dovetailed shape on the ends of the divider. Note that I place a piece of thin plywood over the cutter to make a zero-clearance hole so that the workpiece will be fully supported throughout the cut. Use a push block to safely guide the stock and take equal amounts off each side until it fits in the dove-tailed recess formed in the last step. **(PHOTO B)**

3. Use the tablesaw to cut the grooves in the dividers for the bottom panels. **(PHOTO C)**

4. After adding the bottom panels and installing the miter keys, the boxes will be ready to drill to fit the

magnets. Center the holes in the divider, except for on the bottom box, where the magnet fits the base, and the top box, where the magnet will be made unnecessary by the hinged lid. **(PHOTO D)**

5. Add smaller ³/₁₆-in. diameter magnets centered on the top and bottom of the end of each layer so that when you do want the tower of boxes to align in perfect balance, the magnets will provide the perfect stopping points. The bottom layer and the base must be drilled for magnets using the same technique used in the earlier box.

ROUT THE SIDES between stops in matched pairs for the installation of the dividers. Use a dovetail bit or straight bit. The dovetail adds greater interest.

ROUT BOTH SIDES of the divider.

USE THE TABLESAW to cut grooves in the dividers for the bottom panels.

CUT THE BOTTOM panels to fit, proceed with assembly, and install the magnets at the center of each divider strip.

Design Gallery

ONCE YOU'VE MASTERED THE
BASICS of box making you can
explore using the design elements
and principles in new and creative
ways. There are no limits to what
you can do. What if you add feet?
What if you change the shape of
a pull, or use woods and materials
that one might not expect? I hope
this book serves as an invitation
to have greater confidence in your
own ability to design and make
beautiful boxes.

Don't Overlook the Feet

A single countersunk screw driven through the bottom of a rounded disk foot secures it to the corner of the box.

By cutting away the bottom edge of the sides, the box effectively ends up with four feet.

Cutting away the bottom edge of a base frame also produces feet.

An oversize flat base creates the look of a molding around the bottom of the box.

A Pull Can Push the Envelope

Small lathe turnings make wonderful pulls. A tenon formed on end holds it in place.

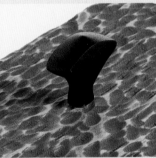

This T-shaped profile quietly invites the thumb and forefingers, and is good for heavier lids.

Rounded and softened edges give this fan-shaped pull a delicate look that works nicely with lightweight lids.

A single bent wire gives a unique look. This one is from Horton Brasses (www.horton-brasses.com).

Mounted to the front of a hinged lid, the pull serves as a lifting point.

The natural curve of a live edge works perfectly as a lift for some boxes.

Flat stock doweled to a pair of posts adds an Asian flavor. Scale the size up or down depending on the box dimensions.

Hinges Can Add Just the Right Touch

This flat shopmade hinge is screwed from underneath.

Wood pins secure an L-shaped shopmade hinge.

Three pieces of leather— two end pieces and a center piece—are secured with brass tacks to create a unique hinge.

Throw a Curve

Curves can help to integrate shapely materials into the con- fines of a rectangular form.

Curving lines combined with straight lines can create a sense of whimsy.

Curves can lighten the look of heavy boxes and make edges more touchable.

Lid Choices Abound

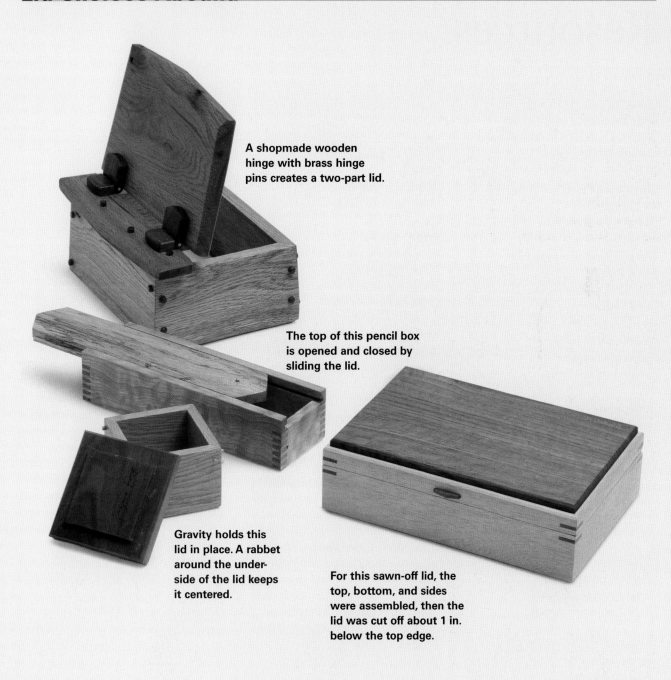

A shopmade wooden hinge with brass hinge pins creates a two-part lid.

The top of this pencil box is opened and closed by sliding the lid.

Gravity holds this lid in place. A rabbet around the underside of the lid keeps it centered.

For this sawn-off lid, the top, bottom, and sides were assembled, then the lid was cut off about 1 in. below the top edge.

Resources

RARE EARTH MAGNETS
K&J Magnetics, Inc.
A full selection of rare earth magnets
www.kjmagnetics.com

HARDWARE FOR BOXMAKING
Lee Valley Tools
www.LeeValley.com

Rockler Woodworking and Hardware
Stores and catalog
www.Rockler.com

Woodcraft Supply
Stores and catalog
www.Woodcraft.com

Hawthorne Crafts
www. HawthorneCrafts.com

Small Box Hardware.com
www. Smallboxhardware.com

Your local hardware store or building supply

VENEERING
Joe Woodworker.com
Information and supplies
www. Joewoodworker.com

GENERAL WOODWORKING INFORMATION
Fine Woodworking
www.Finewoodworking.com

DOUG STOWE'S BOOKS IN PRINT
Available from www.tauntonstore.com
Taunton's Complete Illustrated Guide to Box Making
Basic Box Making
Rustic Furniture Basics
Building Small Cabinets

DOUG STOWE'S DVDS
Available from www.tauntonstore.com
Basic Box Making
Rustic Furniture Basics
Building Small Cabinets

DOUG STOWE'S BLOGS
Boxmaking101.blogspot.com
WisdomofHands.blogspot.com

DOUG STOWE'S WEBSITES
Boxmaking101.com
DougStowe.com

WHERE TO GET WOOD
Where to get wood is the question that my students always ask. I consider the finding and acquisition of wood for building boxes to be one of the great adventures of woodworking. It's an adventure that's led me down narrow country lanes in search of sawmills that offer interesting, beautiful local woods. Would it be right for me to deprive my readers of the adventure that I've enjoyed so much?

You can find wonderful woods for sale on eBay and other websites that can be delivered to your door. But most of the wood I use for making boxes comes from offcuts and leftovers from larger works. I have to admit to being a hoarder of beautiful woods, and because of that, no woods were purchased in the making of this book, or I would have been able to tell you, my dear readers, where to buy. Instead, I will direct you to the best information available for your own small local community.

Look for woodworking clubs in your city or town. I have taught in woodworking clubs all across the U.S. and I've found them to be the Mount Everest of woodworking information. You will be astounded by the willingness of other woodworkers to share sources and materials. I have found amateur woodworkers to be the most generous of our human kind. Whether in a club or not, look for other woodworkers in your community, share what you are learning and your enthusiasm for it, and you will find support, friends, and even free lumber on occasion.

Metric Equivalents

Inches	Centimeters	Millimeters	Inches	Centimeters	Millimeters
⅛	0.3	3	13	33.0	330
¼	0.6	6	14	35.6	356
⅜	1.0	10	15	38.1	381
½	1.3	13	16	40.6	406
⅝	1.6	16	17	43.2	432
¾	1.9	19	18	45.7	457
⅞	2.2	22	19	48.3	483
1	2.5	25	20	50.8	508
1¼	3.2	32	21	53.3	533
1½	3.8	38	22	55.9	559
1¾	4.4	44	23	58.4	584
2	5.1	51	24	61.0	610
2½	6.4	64	25	63.5	635
3	7.6	76	26	66.0	660
3½	8.9	89	27	68.6	686
4	10.2	102	28	71.1	711
4½	11.4	114	29	73.7	737
5	12.7	127	30	76.2	762
6	15.2	152	31	78.7	787
7	17.8	178	32	81.3	813
8	20.3	203	33	83.8	838
9	22.9	229	34	86.4	864
10	25.4	254	35	88.9	889
11	27.9	279	36	91.4	914
12	30.5	305			

If you like this book,
you'll love *Fine Woodworking*.